POLITELY REJECTING
THE BIBLE

POLITELY REJECTING THE BIBLE

Why You Shouldn't Believe Everything the Bible Tells You

DAN KAPR

Enersin Press

Politely Rejecting the Bible: Why You Shouldn't Believe Everything the Bible Tells You

Copyright © 2021 by Dan Kapr

First Printing, December 2021

Book & cover design by Dan Kapr
Cover image: Canva

ISBN 979-8-9853324-1-4 (paperback)
ISBN 979-8-9853324-0-7 (ebook)

www.dankapr.com

A Note for Readers of the E-book

For technical reasons not worth describing, there were unfortunate limitations with setting up footnote links in some versions of the e-book, meaning that you may not be able to easily view the footnotes as you read through the main text. In addition to whatever functionality your e-reader may offer, I have provided one more option. The end notes can be viewed on my website at the following web address:

https://dankapr.com/politely-rejecting-the-bible-notes

This at least gives the reader the option of having the notes readily available in a different screen or window (or even on another device) without having to swipe back and forth in the e-book and risk losing their place. It's not a perfect solution but some readers may find it preferable to the alternatives.

Contents

PART TWO
EXAMINING THE EVIDENCE

Introduction

Every summer when I was little, I attended a weeklong event at my family's church called "Vacation Bible School." At the beginning of each night, we recited the pledge of allegiance to the American flag and the pledge of allegiance to the Christian flag. Then, with one of the children holding up a big leather-bound Bible at the front of the assembly, we recited the final pledge:

> *I pledge allegiance to the Bible,*
> *God's Holy Word.*
> *I will make it a lamp unto my feet,*
> *And a light unto my path*
> *And will hide its words in my heart*
> *That I might not sin against God.*

In hindsight, that does seem like a lot of allegiances for a six-year-old.

Over the course of my childhood, I learned to treat the Bible as the "Word of God." We called it the Word of God because we believed that God was its author, which meant that everything it said was true. The Bible was our guide to knowing about who God was, what he had done for us, and what he was going to do in the future. A good Christian was expected to submit to its instructions and live by its principles. Anyone who denied anything that was taught in the Bible was rebelling against the truth and falling for a

Satanic delusion. I had to be especially careful because—as I learned in church—there were even people who called themselves "Christian" whose doctrines went against biblical teachings.

I began to read the Bible for myself at the age of ten. At the time, I was only allowed to read from the King James Version, which makes it seem all the more remarkable that I read through the entire Pentateuch (Genesis through Deuteronomy), most of the historical books in the Old Testament, the book of Revelation, and three of the Gospels. Revelation held particular interest for me because my Christian community placed a heavy emphasis on the second coming of Jesus Christ and the soon-to-be-realized "end times." It seemed that we had a detailed manual of coming world events, given to us directly by God. This gave us hope that no matter how bad things got, God would always be in control of history, and ultimately he would deliver us from evil.

When I was fourteen, I convinced my parents to let me have a copy of the Bible in a modern English translation. This took my fascination with the Bible to the next level, since now I could make more sense out of what I was reading, and I could read longer portions in one sitting with a better awareness of how it all fit together. My growing familiarity with the Bible also led to a growing familiarity with some of its critics. I learned that non-believers would sometimes explain their rejection of Christianity by talking about the Bible's internal contradictions. This did not bother me because it seemed that these so-called "contradictions" were easy to resolve.

To give one example, the Gospel of Matthew says that when a group of women went to Jesus' tomb they encountered an angel (Matthew 28:1-5), but the Gospel of Luke says that they encountered two angels (Luke 24:1-7). Some critics treat this as a blatant discrepancy, but the solution seemed obvious to me at the time: there were two angels, but Matthew only mentions one of them. After all, if you read Matthew carefully, it never says that there was *only* one angel at the tomb. What was so confusing about that? Skeptics, I told myself, only see errors in the Bible because they want to.

It was not until my last two years at a Christian college that the question of the Bible's accuracy and internal consistency became much more pressing. I was troubled not by the arguments of skeptics but, rather, by the work of conservative evangelical scholars. Evangelical Christians strongly affirm the Bible's authority as a divine revelation, but it seemed that they were willing to admit far more divergence between the Gospels than I was comfortable with. In one evangelical resource, Robert Stein defends the widely held view that the authors of Matthew and Luke used the Gospel of Mark as one of their sources.[1] That did not seem like a problem to me. The part that troubled me was where Stein observes how, when copying a story from Mark, they would sometimes change the wording in order to avoid certain problems created by Mark's narrative.[2]

For instance, in the Gospel of Mark a rich man approaches Jesus and says, "Good Teacher, what must I do to inherit eternal life?" Jesus replies, "Why do you call me good? No one is good but God alone" (Mark 10:17-18). Jesus seems to deny his own goodness, since in that religious framework no human is intrinsically good. This would imply that he is not God—at least, it is easy to read the passage that way. We can see why this might make a Christian reader uncomfortable. The author of Matthew changes the story so that, in his version, the rich man says, "Teacher, what good deed must I do to have eternal life?" to which Jesus replies, "Why do you ask me about what is good?" (Matthew 19:16-17). It seems like the author changed the wording from Mark to avoid a theological difficulty.[3]

Another thing that troubled me in evangelical discourse about the Gospels was the emphasis on Mark's less refined writing style. Daniel Wallace says without hesitation, in a popular Christian resource, that the author of Mark is "one of the worst writers of Greek in the New Testament" and comments on how bad his grammar is.[4]

Stein likewise gives multiple examples of Mark's "inferior" writing, including several instances where the author uses a plural verb with a singular subject or vice versa.[5]

This was all terribly confusing to me. How could the Bible be a divine revelation if the authors were allowed to revise the sayings of Jesus in order to avoid theological difficulties? How could the Word of God have bad grammar? My existing approach to the Bible did not provide any framework for answering these questions, so I could see that something needed to change in my thinking. Either these evangelical scholars were wrong or my view of the Bible lacked the appropriate nuance. Both possibilities made me uncomfortable, but I assumed that my continuing study of the Bible would lead me to a more mature Christian faith.

For most of the next decade I immersed myself deeply in Christian scholarship about the Bible, especially the New Testament, while pursuing a career in ministry. I paid close attention to areas of strong disagreement between evangelical scholars. Whenever I encountered a "difficult" passage in scripture, I would spend significant time studying it and trying to understand what God might be saying through it. Years later I finally concluded that evangelical scholars were indeed wrong, but not in the way I might have anticipated. Their error, I now believed, was in treating the Bible as the Word of God in the first place.

This is not the outcome I expected, nor the one I wanted. The thought of having in my possession a written revelation from God was a source of great comfort to me. When I ultimately rejected this idea, it was a devastating personal loss. I went through a serious grieving process. My confidence in the Bible's divine origin gave me a strong sense of stability, even if that sense was an illusion. To know that I could spend the rest of my life consulting this resource and learning more about God's will and his control over history—that was not something I could easily part with. In addition to my fear of losing that sense of stability, I was also afraid of making a serious mistake and putting myself in disfavor with God. Frankly, I was terrified of what would happen if I got things wrong. I suppose it did not help that I was halfway through a seminary degree and working at a Baptist church.

In spite of these concerns, I had to be honest with myself. It now seemed painfully clear to me that my whole worldview up until that point had been rooted in a false teaching. Contrary to what I had always believed, the Bible is not an authoritative, perfect source of truth. It contains many falsehoods—not just historical inaccuracies, but moral and theological errors as well. While this did not destroy my Christian faith (that happened later, for other reasons), it did require a major overhaul in my personal life. Since I no longer regarded the Bible as a revelation from God, I felt uncomfortable attending church services where we publicly proclaimed it as such. I had been taught my whole life to take the truth about God seriously. It did not seem wise to suddenly ignore that principle.

In this book I will explain why I changed my mind about the Bible. I will spend the first half of the book exploring the idea that the Bible contains no falsehoods. The concept seems simple enough, but upon closer inspection it turns out to be surprisingly complicated. Christians have always affirmed the truthfulness of the Bible in ways that might seem counterintuitive, and even today Christians who believe in the Bible's "inerrancy," as it is called, have significant disagreements about what would constitute a true error in scripture. In order to assess this approach to the Bible, we must make sure we understand it.

In the second half of the book I will examine a handful of passages in which the Bible makes demonstrably false claims. I limited myself to a small number of cases because I wanted to give each one a sufficient amount of attention, rather than cataloguing a large number of biblical errors while only making a few comments about each. I know from experience that the latter approach does not change many minds. The advantage of focusing more intently on just a handful of cases is that it allowed me to select some of the most compelling examples that I could think of. These range from minor historical errors to major theological falsehoods.

My aim is to offer as much insight as possible about why approaching the Bible as an infallible source of truth fails on its own terms. My hope is that this book will motivate readers to grant these matters the weight that they deserve and, if necessary, to adjust their worldview accordingly. This is not meant to be a hostile attack on anyone's cherished personal beliefs. Rather, it is a plea for a more rigorous and thoughtful engagement with issues that have a profound impact on our world. The Bible's role in Christianity is a topic of great personal significance, and I had many friends and loved ones in mind as I wrote, especially those who I know will probably disagree with me but who I hope will find the discussion interesting and perhaps even persuasive. For that reason I have labored hard to keep the tone as civil as possible.

I am lucky to have become friends with some truly wonderful people since going through the difficult process of leaving my old religious environment, including others who have also rejected the things they learned as children in the evangelical church. I am grateful for their presence in my life. In particular, I want to express my sincerest gratitude to Jen Kane and Mandy Robinson, who graciously read through the entire manuscript and provided helpful feedback. The book is stronger for it, and I take full credit for any mistakes or weak points that remain.

PART ONE

Preliminary Inquiries

Chapter One

What Is Biblical Inerrancy?

"All scripture is inspired by God," writes one early Christian author, and as a result it is "useful for teaching, for reproof, for correction, and for training in righteousness."[1] The concept of inspiration plays a crucial role in current Christian debates about the Bible. I am not aware of any Christian group that denies the inspiration of scripture, but there is no consensus about what it means for a text to be inspired. In modern discourse, the word "inspiration" is frequently used in reference to exceptional moments of creativity or insight. But Christians typically see the Bible as something more than just a brilliant human achievement.

The Greek word translated as "inspired" in the passage above literally means "God-breathed." In the Old Testament, which contains the Jewish scriptures, the breath of God is associated with the Spirit of God, and the Spirit of God is what allows prophets to reveal divine oracles.[2] For this reason, another early Christian author explains that "no prophecy was ever made by an act of human will, but men moved by the Holy Spirit spoke from God."[3]

In this context, to say that scripture is inspired is to affirm that God played some kind of role in the writing process, resulting in a text that functions as a divine revelation. Philo of Alexandria, a

Jewish philosopher who lived around the same time as Jesus, speaks about prophets being "possessed" by divine inspiration, such that they become sounding instruments of God's voice, "being struck and moved to sound in an invisible manner by him."[4] The first-century Jewish historian Flavius Josephus talks about inspiration as a process by which prophets learn directly from God, and he describes the Jewish scriptures as "divine."[5]

The concept of inspiration is closely related to the Bible's authority. If the human authors of the Bible wrote by divine inspiration, then in a literal sense God is the true author of scripture. As the "Word of God," the Bible has authority over the people of God, because in it God tells them what to believe and how to live. Many Christians believe that if the Bible is an inspired and authoritative revelation from God, then it cannot contain any mistakes or contradictions at all, since everything God says is true. This is the doctrine of biblical inerrancy, which holds that the Bible is "inerrant," or free from error.

Some Christians accept the traditional understanding of the Bible's inspiration and authority, but fall short of affirming its full or "unlimited" inerrancy. Instead, they allow room for minor errors and discrepancies. Those who take this approach often say that the Bible is true in everything it says with regard to theological and moral teachings, even though it may get certain details wrong when it comes to history and science. Sometimes they prefer to describe the Bible as "infallible" rather than "inerrant," although depending on the context these two terms can be synonymous.[6] Other Christians speak of the Bible's "limited inerrancy," a paradoxical term which means that God only prevented the human writers from making mistakes in regard to certain matters, such as theology.[7]

Christians also take a variety of approaches to the concept of inspiration. Some Christians affirm the Bible's "plenary" inspiration, meaning that every part of the Bible is inspired, and its "verbal" inspiration, meaning that every word of the Bible is inspired.[8] These views on inspiration pair nicely with biblical inerrancy. Other Christians reject these doctrines in favor of a view which upholds the inspiration of scripture while claiming that it does not apply to all parts of scripture equally.[9] The common underlying conviction for all of these views is that, in some sense, the biblical writings (or at least parts of them) had a divine origin.

Then there are other Christians who go further and deny the Bible's divine origin altogether. They see errors and contradictions in scripture as an indication that God did not guide the human writers at all, resulting in a much different view of inspiration and authority. On this view, the Bible is a fully human text, reflecting a variety of conflicting human perspectives, but the writings are all grounded in a genuine experience of God. The Bible's authority relates more to the fact that Christians must remain in constant dialogue with this particular set of writings. These writings give Christians a vocabulary for speaking about God, and they help to mark out the community in which that vocabulary makes sense. The Bible is sacred, not because it came from God, but because of its origin as a human response to the reality of God and because of the role it has played in Christian history. Christians may conclude that certain parts of the Bible are deeply in error, but they cannot reject those parts of the Bible as scripture without ceasing to be Christian.[10]

In this book, I will be focusing on the idea that the Bible is a divine product, with a particular emphasis on the doctrine of inerrancy. If the Bible is inerrant, then we must believe everything it says. On the other hand, if it does contain errors, then believing everything it says would be a serious mistake. In that case, we will want to get a sense of just how wrong the Bible can be. While the question of whether the biblical writings are rooted in a genuine experience of God is interesting, it will not concern us here.

It is important to keep in mind that doctrines regarding the Bible's inerrancy or infallibility are not essential to Christian faith. Many people worship Jesus and embrace a Christian worldview without believing everything the Bible says. To disprove inerrancy is not to disprove Christianity. This should not be too controversial, since the earliest Christians practiced their faith before any of the New Testament books were written. It would be strange if the validity of their faith depended on the credibility of books that did not yet exist. Even so, the inerrancy of scripture is affirmed in various ways by a large number of Christians, and many churches treat inerrancy as an essential doctrine.

A Modern Doctrine

Prior to the nineteenth century, no one spoke about "the doctrine of inerrancy" or referred to the Bible as "inerrant." That doesn't mean that Christians never addressed the subject of errors in the Bible until then, but the terminology was new, as was the context in which it developed. Part of the reason this development occurred when it did was because of the intellectual climate in North America at that time.

One of the prevailing philosophies was a view called "empiricism," which holds that knowledge is derived from experience—more specifically, from what we perceive through our physical senses. This view was a conscious rejection of a different philosophy called "rationalism," which held that knowledge is based on innate ideas that we bring with us to our experience. Empiricists claimed that science does not impose any pre-existing theory on the empirical (observable) data. Instead, it merely observes and classifies the data, and forms generalizations on the basis of those observations.

Owing to the influence of these ideas, some Christians began to treat the Bible as a repository of facts that one could properly analyze without imposing any pre-existing theoretical framework. Just as empiricists believed that knowledge is based purely on data derived from experience, many Christians believed that knowledge of doctrinal truth is based purely on the data derived from the biblical text. The "facts" of scripture were plain to anyone who would look, and one only needed to classify them.[11]

It was in this context that the fundamentalist movement was born. Nowadays the word "fundamentalism" refers broadly to dogmatic or anti-intellectual ways of thinking, so that one can even speak of atheist fundamentalism. However, it originally referred specifically to a Christian movement from the early twentieth century which declined significantly after the famous Scopes Monkey Trial in 1925.

Fundamentalism was largely an American Protestant reaction to modern science (especially Darwinism and evolutionary theory) and to modern biblical criticism (especially historical criticism of the Gospels).[12] These academic trends had created an atmosphere that was favorable to a more liberal version of Christianity, which denied the miracles of the Bible and regarded Jesus as an enlightened moral teacher rather than a miracle-working savior who died for the sins of the world. Fundamentalists responded by reasserting their belief in the "fundamentals" of Christian faith. These fundamentals were famously expressed as five key doctrines: the virgin birth, the atonement, the bodily resurrection of Jesus, the authenticity of the biblical miracles, and the inerrancy of scripture.[13] Before long, the doctrine of inerrancy became associated with a strict literalist interpretation of the Bible, especially the creation stories in the book of Genesis.[14]

It is important to note the distinctly Protestant nature of the movement. While fundamentalists believed that the Bible's authority was under attack from modern scholarship, they also believed that it was being threatened by the Roman Catholic Church. In addition to describing scripture as "inerrant," they also used the term "infallible" as a way of challenging a relatively new Catholic emphasis on the infallibility of the pope.[15]

Before the rise of fundamentalism, conservative Christian leaders could openly acknowledge imperfections in the Bible. For example, in 1899, a conservative Baptist pastor named Robert MacArthur gave a defense of traditional Christian theology in which he said, "A true doctrine of inspiration may admit mistakes, or at least the possibility of mistakes, in history and biographical statements, while it denies error in matters of faith and morals."[16] Additionally, conservative church leaders were not always strictly attached to anti-Darwinist interpretations of the Bible.[17] Many of them had happily embraced Darwin's theory. In fact, one of the key leaders of the fundamentalist movement, Benjamin B. Warfield, supported the idea of biological evolution.[18]

Perhaps it is understandable why many Christians reject the doctrine of biblical inerrancy today. After all, it is a relatively recent doctrine developed by Christians within the framework of a modernist philosophy. In that light, it is easy to see inerrancy as a deviation from more traditional Christian approaches to scripture. However, it would be wrong to think that nobody worried about errors or contradictions in the Bible up until this point in history. The basic concept behind the doctrine of inerrancy—the idea that the Bible's authors did not err in what they wrote—is hardly a modern innovation. It is as ancient as Christianity itself. We can see this for ourselves by turning to the writings of Augustine of Hippo.

An Ancient Principle

If anyone has a claim to be the most influential theologian in the history of the Western church, surely Augustine does. Born in Africa in the fourth century CE, he became the bishop of Hippo (located in modern-day Algeria) in 395. He spent the rest of his life writing numerous works on Christian theology and addressing various controversies in the church. His writings played a major role in shaping mainstream Christian thought concerning topics as important as the Trinity and the relationship between God's grace and human choice.[19] Writing about fifteen hundred years prior to the rise of fundamentalism, Augustine's approach to scripture is worth considering.

In his *Reply to Faustus the Manichaean*, Augustine directly addresses the question of biblical authority. First, he draws a distinction between "our writings"—that is, his own writings and those of other church leaders—and the writings of the Bible. His own writings are meant for the edification of the church, and he admits that they may contain mistakes that need to be corrected. But the situation is different when it comes to the Old and New Testaments:

> The authority of these books has come down to us from the apostles through the successions of bishops and the extension of the Church, and, from a position of lofty supremacy, claims the submission of every faithful and pious mind. If we are perplexed by an apparent contradiction in Scripture, it is not allowable to say, The author of this book is mistaken; but either the manuscript is faulty, or the translation is wrong, or you have not understood.[20]

In a letter to Jerome (another important figure in church history),

Augustine makes a similar statement. Regarding the scriptures, he says, "I have learned to yield this respect and honour only to the canonical books of Scripture: of these alone do I most firmly believe that the authors were completely free from error."[21]

This testimony from Augustine is a powerful indication that referring to biblical inerrancy as a modern doctrine without providing further context is misleading. The idea that scripture is free from error (which is, after all, what the word "inerrant" means) has been around for a long time. Of course, this idea was not worked out in detail or proclaimed as an essential Christian doctrine prior to the fundamentalist movement. This is why earlier Christian theologians could hold a more flexible view of the Bible.

Augustine would not necessarily have agreed with what we now call the doctrine of inerrancy. Ancient Christians, including Augustine, generally took a much different approach to interpreting the Bible from that of modern day "inerrantists," as believers in inerrancy are called. In fact, it was their commitment to affirming the truth of scripture that led many ancient theologians to embrace ways of understanding scripture that would strike a contemporary reader as quite strange. This is something we will explore later. Nevertheless, the idea that the Bible does not err in what it says is not a modern invention.

In fact, this idea goes back even earlier than Augustine to the very roots of the church. Here it is important to remember that Christianity began in the first century CE as a Jewish movement.[22] Christian writings from that time attest to the difficult relationship between the growing Christian community and the wider Jewish world, especially as the church added more and more gentiles to its numbers. Ultimately, there was a breaking point, and it became clear that Christianity was now a distinct religion in its own right, and no longer a Jewish movement. Yet Christianity retained a number of Judaism's features, including its dependence on sacred books for guidance in belief and practice.

It may seem natural to us that different religions should each have their own holy books, but this "bookishness" was not a common feature of other religions at the time.[23] Although the exact limits of Jewish scripture may not have been defined until after the birth of Christianity,[24] written scripture already played a crucial role in Judaism long before Jesus was born. Not only that, but Jewish and Christian writings from roughly the third century BCE through the first few centuries CE were largely preoccupied with interpreting or creatively rewriting scripture in light of present events.

We can see instances of this within the Old Testament itself. For example, the book of Daniel offers a stunning reinterpretation of a prophecy from the book of Jeremiah. Whereas Jeremiah had predicted that the Jewish people would be in exile for seventy years, it was now "revealed" to Daniel that the punishment of exile would last for seventy "weeks" or "sevens" of years, that is, four hundred and ninety years (see Daniel 9:1-3, 20-27).

The Jewish and Christian literature from this period reflects a wide variety of perspectives. These writings played a major role in shaping the way that the Bible has been understood down through the centuries. Many of the things we associate with the Bible do not actually come from the Bible itself, but rather from the Bible's ancient interpreters.

For instance, ancient Jews and Christians identified the talking serpent in the story of Adam and Eve as Satan, but the Bible never explicitly makes this connection (although it may be implied in the book of Revelation[25]). Still, for most Christians this tradition is so familiar that it *is* part of the Bible. It may even seem like a natural and obvious way to read the story in Genesis. Yet it only seems this way because the interpretation has become widely embraced over the course of time. Some ancient interpreters saw the talking serpent as an indication that, prior to Adam and Eve's disobedience, all animals could talk. On that view, the talking serpent was, quite literally, just a regular snake engaging in conversation with a human. It was because of the snake's deceitfulness that God took its speech away.[26]

In spite of the diversity of ancient interpretations of scripture, they all seem to be grounded in certain shared assumptions. One of these common underlying assumptions is that all inspired scripture is perfectly harmonious—in other words, free of contradictions. Josephus says of Jewish scripture, "For we have not an innumerable multitude of books among us, disagreeing from and contradicting one another [as the Greeks have] but only twenty-two books, which contain the records of all past times; which are justly believed to be divine."[27]

The assumption of scripture's perfect harmony is reflected in the way that ancient interpreters deal with discrepancies found in scripture. Since they believed that all scripture speaks with a single voice, they attempted to reconcile the discrepancies in ingenious ways. Often they did this by drawing wisdom from one part of scripture and applying it to a completely different, seemingly unrelated passage.[28]

This ancient approach to resolving discrepancies in scripture bears a strong resemblance to the way some Christians defend the Bible's inerrancy today. In some cases, Christians still use arguments that were originally developed by ancient writers. For instance, in Genesis 1:26, when God creates human beings, he says, "Let us make humankind in our image, according to our likeness." This seems strange since Judaism and Christianity both insist that there is only one God. So who is God talking to when he says "Let *us* make humankind in *our* image"? How can there be only one God if God was helped in creation by someone else? Ancient interpreters came up with different answers.

One explanation comes from a Jewish source called *Genesis*

Rabba, an anthology of rabbinic comments compiled in the fourth or fifth century CE. In one passage, Rabbi Hanina says, "When God set out to create the first human, He consulted with the ministering angels. He said to them, 'Let us make man.'"[29] The "us" in Genesis 1:26 refers to God and the angels. Certain evangelicals still take this approach, as seen in the *NIV Study Bible*.[30]

Some ancient Christian sources give a different explanation. The *Letter of Barnabus*, which was probably written in the second century CE, says that it was "the Lord of all the earth," here referring to Jesus, "to whom at the foundation of the world God had addressed the words, Let us make man, in our own image and likeness."[31] This is the view defended in the *ESV Study Bible*.[32] In many ways, modern Christian views of the Bible are rooted in ancient views of scripture.

According to the New Testament, Jesus also believed that scripture, rightly interpreted, was free of contradiction. To explain this, some background information is needed. There was a widespread belief in first-century Judaism that someday God was going to defeat the Jewish people's enemies for good, at which time God would raise his people from the dead and reward them with a new, glorious life. They called this event "the resurrection." One Jewish group known as the Sadducees did not believe in the resurrection, probably because they only accepted the Pentateuch (the first five books of the Bible) as authoritative scripture.[33] The Pentateuch does not say anything about the resurrection. In fact, it does not seem to envision any sort of afterlife at all. But some of the later biblical writings accepted by the wider Jewish community do speak about resurrection.[34]

In the Gospel of Mark, the Sadducees challenge Jesus' belief in the resurrection. They say, "Teacher, Moses wrote for us that if a man's brother dies, leaving a wife but no child, the man shall marry the widow and raise up children for his brother" (Mark 12:19). Here they are referring to the custom of levirate marriage, which is described in Deuteronomy 25:5. The Sadducees then present Jesus with the following scenario:

> There were seven brothers; the first married and, when he died, left no children; and the second married the widow and died, leaving no children; and the third likewise; none of the seven left children. Last of all the woman herself died. In the resurrection whose wife will she be? For the seven had married her. (Mark 12:20-23)

They think this refutes the doctrine of the resurrection because it implies what they see as an absurd scenario—namely, that after everyone is raised from the dead, the woman will have seven husbands. In their minds, this conflicts with what scripture says, and the implication is that what scripture says cannot be false.

Jesus responds by saying, "Is not this the reason you are wrong, that you know neither the scriptures nor the power of God?" He denies that marriage will still exist after the resurrection, and quotes a passage from the Pentateuch, interpreting it in such a way as to show that resurrection has been part of God's plan all along (Mark 12:24-27). His interpretation will probably seem counterintuitive to modern readers, but the important thing to notice here is that Jesus is harmonizing the Pentateuch with the other scriptures that speak of resurrection. None of this would make sense if either Jesus or the Sadducees thought that the scriptures could contradict each other.

It seems that the ancient interpreters of scripture are operating with what we might call a principle of inerrancy. In other words, they assume that scripture does not contain errors or contradictions. But we must be careful not to overstate this point. Some Christian theologians, such as John Chrysostom and Origen, were comfortable with suggesting that there might be disagreements on peripheral details in the biblical writings, while maintaining that they were perfectly unified in their doctrinal and moral teaching.[35] Additionally, the early church routinely interpreted scripture in non-literal ways, and their understanding of the "true" meaning of scripture would not necessarily be affected by what modern evangelicals consider to be errors.[36]

The idea that scripture is free of falsehood and contradiction is an ancient one indeed. It is reflected in the recorded teachings of Jesus, and it unquestionably plays a significant role in the history of Christian theology and biblical interpretation. On the other hand, the *doctrine* of inerrancy, as it is known today, has only been around for less than two centuries, and it has a decidedly modern flavor. Sometimes, when we talk about the Bible's inerrancy or infallibility, we are talking about a modern doctrine which imposes an interpretation on scripture that would not have mattered as much to ancient Christians. In other cases, we are talking about the way scripture has been understood since the time of Jesus and the early church.

Chapter Two

How Do We Know What the Bible Says?

In order to discuss the Bible's credibility as a divinely inspired text, we need to know what the Bible says. Unfortunately, I have heard a number of people express skepticism about whether we can know what the biblical authors actually wrote. It is not just that there are seemingly endless versions of the Bible to choose from. There is also the fact that the books of the Bible were written such a long time ago, and then they were passed down to us by communities with strong vested interests in safeguarding their religious doctrines. It is easy to think that the texts were probably distorted beyond recognition, perhaps even manipulated to make them conform to Christian dogma. If we do not know what the authors wrote down, this means we probably cannot say much about Jesus or early Christianity.

This kind of skepticism is understandable, but it is far too hasty. People in the ancient world were well aware that texts could be corrupted, and some Christian leaders expressed frustration when the biblical writings were copied or translated incorrectly.[1] It was precisely their faith in the text's inspiration that drove their concern to know what it really said. Of course, there are plenty of cases where people have forged or altered a text out of religious zeal.[2] Neverthe-less, a religious bias does not guarantee the corruption of a sacred text.

A blanket denial of our ability to know the authentic text of the Bible due to its antiquity is more radical than many people realize. If such reasoning were sound, it would not just affect our knowledge of the Bible. On the contrary, it would undermine all of our knowl-edge about the ancient world. This is because our understanding of the past relies heavily on ancient books that have far less textual support than the Bible does. (I will explain what "textual support" means later in the chapter.) Some might be tempted to embrace this radical conclusion and claim that historical knowledge is impossi-ble. This position entails, among other things, that we could never be sure of what words an ancient author wrote down. If this were true, there would be no point in writing a book like this, since we would be incapable of learning anything about the past—except, I suppose, for the fact that it cannot be learned.

A recurring problem with extreme forms of skepticism is that they usually turn out to be self-defeating: "I know that knowledge is unobtainable," "The truth about reality is that we cannot say any-thing true about reality," and so on. Radical skepticism is also seem-ingly impossible to maintain in a consistent manner. Imagine trying to defend the position of historical skepticism without offering any reconstruction of past events. You could not appeal to the problems that historians have previously encountered in their work, nor could you explain how any particular theory was developed.

We saw that some people doubt that we can know what the Bible originally said, because it was written such a long time ago and was handed down by communities with strong religious biases. But even this argument suffers from a lack of consistency. How do we know that it was "a long time ago"? How do we know what communities were involved in preserving the texts, or what religious beliefs they held? Even to present the skeptical view, one has to claim an awful lot of historical knowledge. And any knowledge of what was going on in the ancient world is inevitably grounded in the testimony of ancient writers. If we cannot trust these sources, then the argument for doubting the integrity of the biblical text has no ground; and if we can trust at least some of what we learn from these sources, then we should not throw out the text of the Bible without carefully examining it.

My goal here is not to offer a broad defense of historical knowledge. Rather, I want to explain why debates about the Bible are not a complete waste of time. In that sense, I am defending one specific historical claim. We really can possess knowledge about what the biblical authors wrote, but the way we come to possess this knowledge is more complicated than simply opening up a Bible and seeing what it says.

An English-speaking person's ability to know what the Bible says depends crucially on two disciplines. The first discipline is translation, since the books of the Bible were originally written in Hebrew, Aramaic, and Greek. The second discipline is textual criticism, since the original writings, called "autographs," no longer exist, meaning that the text of the Bible must be reconstructed from later copies. Without the work of reliable translators and textual critics, we would have no idea what the biblical authors actually wrote.

Translation

Although translation might seem like a straightforward process, it can be quite complicated, especially when dealing with ancient languages. For instance, translators must decide what to do with certain expressions that made perfect sense in their original context but would sound confusing in modern English. Should they just translate the text literally? Or is it technically more accurate to interpret the words for the modern reader? A literal translation of 1 Kings 16:11 says that when Zimri killed everyone in the royal family of Baasha, "he didn't spare anyone who urinates on a wall."[3] To modern ears, the sudden mention of urination is baffling, but in its ancient context it made perfect sense. The author was using a Hebrew idiom for referring to males, which is why most modern translations simply say "males."

Sometimes, ancient authors make use of multiple meanings of a word in a way that cannot be expressed in English. This happens in John 3:3-4, where Jesus uses a phrase in Greek that can mean either "born again" or "born from above." This double-meaning plays an important role in the passage since it becomes a point of confusion for Jesus' conversation partner. Unfortunately, we do not have an expression in English that captures this double meaning, so something unavoidably gets lost in translation.

In other cases, the Bible uses a phrase whose meaning is not discernible, making it much harder to translate. We can see a good example of this by comparing different translations of Ecclesiastes 5:9:

> But all things considered, this is an advantage for a land: a king for a plowed field.[4]

> The increase from the land is taken by all; the king himself profits from the fields.[5]

In the original language, it is not clear what the author is trying to say, which is why there is a disparity between the different translations.

For reasons like these, a perfect English translation of the Bible seems impossible even in theory. Each translator has their own opinions about how to handle these kinds of issues and how to work out their principles on a case-by-case basis. For some issues, there is no single right answer (technically "those who urinate on walls" and "males" are both accurate translations of the idiom in 1 Kings 16:11), although there are certainly wrong answers (the idiom should not be translated as "Canadians").

The fact that there is no single right way to translate ancient writings is an inescapable result of the complexity of human language. There are too many points at which a translation must be guided by the needs of the intended audience and by the judgment or aesthetic preferences of the translators. Translators can disagree with each other, and sometimes, in spite of their best judgment, they can make mistakes.

Christians typically agree that some translations are better than others, and that the best way to know what the Bible says is to compare different translations and, if possible, to study the Bible in its original languages. However, a dissenting minority of Protestants believes that a perfect translation of the Bible does exist, namely, the King James Version, which was first published in 1611. For those who are unfamiliar with the "King James Only" movement, this might seem odd. Why should a centuries-old rendering of the text be considered not just superior, but perfect?

One common talking point among King James Only Christians is that modern translations remove verses from the Bible, and therefore cannot be trusted.[6] For example, if you read through the Gospel of Matthew in a contemporary translation, such as the New Revised Standard Version, you will notice that Matthew 17:21 is missing. It just skips from verse 20 to verse 22. You will also see a footnote at the end of verse 20, leading to this comment: "Other ancient authorities add verse 21. . . ." But in the King James Bible, verse 21 is included in the main body of the text, and there are no footnotes providing alternate readings.

If you read the preface of any modern translation, you will find some comments from the translation committee explaining why certain translation decisions were made. Usually, the translators are aware that the final product will be less than perfect, though obviously they are aiming to be as faithful to the text as possible. By contrast, you will not find a preface in your copy of the King James Bible. So, why do modern Bible translations have footnotes and missing verses? This is where textual criticism comes into play.

Textual Criticism

The books contained in the Bible were all written long before the invention of the printing press. In order to be widely disseminated, the texts had to be copied by hand.[7] There was always a possibility that a copyist could make a mistake when producing a new manuscript. Even worse, a copyist could intentionally change, add, or remove material.[8]

This was such a persistent problem with literature in the ancient world that authors would sometimes directly address the copyists to encourage them to faithfully preserve the text, or perhaps threaten them with a curse if they did not.[9] An example of this even shows up in the Bible, at the end of the book of Revelation:

> I warn everyone who hears the words of the prophecy of this book: if anyone adds to them, God will add to that person the plagues described in this book; if anyone takes away from the words of the book of this prophecy, God will take away that person's share in the tree of life and in the holy city, which are described in this book. (Revelation 22:18-19)

In spite of tense warnings like these, changes still made their way into the texts. In fact, the last verse of Revelation, which appears very shortly after the quoted passage, has multiple readings attested in the surviving manuscripts.

Because of these textual changes, we now have a large number of manuscripts for the New Testament books with numerous differences, or "variants," between them.[10] Since the original writings no longer exist, scholars must try to determine which variants most likely reflect the original wording. It is important to note that we have a far greater number of manuscripts for the New Testament than we do for other ancient books.[11] Of course, a greater number of manuscripts means a greater number of variants. The full count of variants in the surviving manuscripts is staggering, numbering in the hundreds of thousands.[12] But strange as it sounds, this is a good thing. An abundance of manuscripts means an abundance of copies to compare against each other. This allows scholars to identify certain trends, which helps in understanding the history of the text.

An analogy from science is helpful here. Every living organism has genes containing DNA. Random mutations cause slight changes in DNA, which can cause physiological changes in an organism. If a physiological change does not impede survival, then when the organism reproduces, the genetic change will be passed down to its offspring. If enough changes accrue over a long period time, then eventually there will be a genetic descendant that looks quite different from the original organism.

If a scribe copies a manuscript of the Bible, they may (purposely or by accident) introduce "mutations" into the text. Now suppose another scribe copies the first scribe's copy. It is easy to see how changes made in the first copy may be preserved in the second copy. If each new copy is then copied in succession, we can imagine more and more changes appearing in the copied text over time. Eventually there will be a whole line of manuscript "descendants," with the final manuscript containing many differences from the original manuscript.

In our biological scenario, if the original organism is a member of a whole species, then there are many opportunities for the DNA to replicate itself, which means more chances for slight variations to occur. Over time, genetic lines may split off from each other, resulting in descendants who look different not only from the original ancestor, but from each other as well. In a similar way, if an original manuscript is copied by two scribes, and then each of their copies is copied, and so on, we can imagine this resulting in two separate lines of manuscripts. At a certain point, the manuscripts in one line will look significantly different not just from the original but also from the manuscripts in the other line.

The analogy with DNA is not perfect. If a scribe makes an obvious mistake when copying a manuscript, it is entirely possible for the next scribe to catch the error and correct it while copying the scribe's copy. Furthermore, a scribe might consult different manuscripts when producing their own copy, meaning that their copy will not neatly reflect one single "line of descent." But the important point to keep in mind is that when scholars compare various manuscripts to each other, certain patterns will emerge in the variants, allowing them to discern "family resemblances" in manuscripts that reflect similar changes.[13]

This is why a massive collection of manuscripts with a massive number of variants is a blessing rather than a curse, at least if we want to get as close to the original wording as possible. By organizing manuscripts based on significant family resemblances, scholars can identify different "text types." There are three major text types for the New Testament.[14] By studying these text types in excruciating detail, scholars can draw firm conclusions about the history of the text. This is what I meant when I spoke earlier of the Bible's superior textual support, especially in regard to the New Testament, since many ancient works only survive in one or two copies. We are in a much better position to know what the New Testament says than we are when it comes to other ancient works.[15]

With the Old Testament, there are fewer manuscripts and fewer variants. Because of this, scholars have less opportunity to determine the likely original wording by comparing different manuscripts to each other. As a result, Old Testament textual criticism proceeds along somewhat different lines than New Testament textual criticism. Reconstructing the original text is based more on dealing with peculiarities that come up in the text, even though they may appear in all known manuscripts.[16] This process involves a fair amount of "conjectural emendation," which is when a scholar proposes a reading not found in any manuscript but which seems like the most likely reading on other grounds.[17] This is not done in a haphazard fashion but in accord with carefully worked out principles in a peer-reviewed setting.

We can see why textual variants can be helpful for establishing the original text. Still, to have hundreds of thousands of variants in the manuscripts of the New Testament seems a bit overwhelming. Thankfully, it is not nearly as bad as it sounds. In the vast majority of cases, the variants have no impact on the meaning of the text. Most of them involve spelling errors or grammatical differences that can't even be translated into English.[18]

Among the minority of cases where the variant affects the meaning, most have no plausible claim to reflect the original text, such as when a variant is only found in a single late manuscript.[19] Among the smaller minority of cases where the variant is meaningful *and* potentially preserves the original wording, the impact on the text's meaning is usually not significant. For instance, should 1 John 1:4 say, "We are writing these things so that *our* joy may be complete," or, "We are writing these things so that *your* joy may be complete"? The answer is uncertain, but it does not make much of a difference.[20]

Of course, some variants have a more significant impact on the text. The two biggest examples are the ending of the Gospel of Mark (Mark 16:9-20) and the story of the woman caught in adultery, found in the Gospel of John (John 7:53-8:11). However, according to most biblical scholars, these passages were not part of the original writings. Other passages which are usually deemed inauthentic include the traditional ending of the Lord's Prayer found in Matthew 6:13 ("For the kingdom and the power and the glory are yours forever. Amen.") and Luke 22:44, where Jesus sweats drops of blood while praying to God.

Scholars have different methods for reconstructing the earliest version of the text, but in some cases (as we saw with 1 John 1:4), they are not able to decide which of two variant readings is more likely to reflect the original. Most contemporary translations use footnotes to show alternate readings supported by different manuscripts. These are the "ancient authorities" mentioned above. To make things a bit more confusing, the chapter and verse numbers in the Bible were not part of the original writings. They were added much later, at a time when there were already lots of manuscripts in existence. When the verse numbers were added, they were sometimes assigned to portions of the text that scholars later identified as inauthentic, such as Matthew 17:21.

The reason contemporary translations differ so much from the King James Bible, in ways that go beyond just updating the words to modern English, is that in the centuries since it was first published, more manuscripts were discovered (including the Dead Sea Scrolls, which were found in the 1940s), leading to revised conclusions about the original biblical text.[21] In particular, the King James Bible relies heavily on a text type that is no longer given the same weight that it once was. This is why certain verses from the King James Bible are omitted in modern translations, though the omitted verses are usually preserved in footnotes.

Many Christians feel the same way about textual criticism as they do about translation: it is a human process, subject to human error. For this reason, inerrantists often clarify that the Bible is only free from error *in the original writings*.[22] It is perfectly possible for copies of the Bible to deviate from what was written in the autographs. They conclude that copies of the Bible can only be inspired and inerrant to the extent that they accurately reflect the original words of scripture.[23] Obviously, this view of inerrancy does not work unless textual criticism is reliable enough to reproduce the autographs with a high degree of accuracy. It would seem odd to insist that a set of writings were free from error if one could not be sure of what those writings originally said.

Whether the doctrine of inerrancy is true or not, there is no serious doubt that the text of the Bible (and especially the New Testament) is indeed established with a high degree of accuracy. You can see this for yourself by getting a modern translation of the Bible and looking through the footnotes. Although some of the textual issues are fascinating, you might be shocked at how insignificant most of them turn out to be.

To drive the point home, let me quote from a biblical scholar named Bart Ehrman. Back when I was in college, Ehrman published a book called *Misquoting Jesus* that caused a firestorm of controversy, because it gave many people the impression that we could not know what the biblical authors originally wrote.[24] This was based on a somewhat reactionary (or perhaps overzealous) misreading of his book. In a later book, Ehrman says quite clearly that in spite of the many variants that exist in the New Testament manuscripts, "the problem is not of such a scope as to make it impossible to have any idea what the ancient Christian authors wrote." Addressing the objection that we have no clue what was originally in the writings of Paul or the Gospels, he observes that "there is not a textual critic on the planet who thinks this, since not a shred of evidence leads in this direction." He concludes, "As a result, in the vast majority of cases, the wording of these authors is not in dispute."[25]

Assessing the King James Only View

Proponents of the King James Only view believe that modern scholars misrepresent the history of the biblical text, and claim that the manuscript tradition behind the King James Bible is far superior to those manuscripts on which modern translations are based.[26] In other words, they do not just believe that it is a better translation, but also that it is the only English translation which reliably preserves the correct words of scripture. On such a view, all other translations are severe distortions of the sacred text because they are working from defective copies. As a result, we have two very different ways of handling the doctrine of biblical inerrancy. One view holds that only the original writings, which no longer exist, were inspired and therefore inerrant. The other view holds that a perfect copy of the original Bible still exists in a particular seventeenth-century English translation.

This disagreement plays an important role in how Christians respond to specific challenges to inerrancy. For example, in 1 Samuel 17, we learn about how David, the future king of Israel, successfully killed a Philistine soldier named Goliath. Yet 2 Samuel 21:19 says that Goliath was killed, not by David, but by a man named Elhanan. Outside of the conservative Christian world, this is usually taken as an indication that the Bible preserves two conflicting traditions about the death of Goliath.[27] Evangelicals typically deal with the problem by appealing to somewhat complicated theories about how the original text was transmitted.[28] However, in the King James Bible, the verse in 2 Samuel does not say that Elhanan killed Goliath, but rather that he killed Goliath's brother. If the King James Only view is correct, then there is no discrepancy to deal with, at least not in this case.

Obviously, the Bible does not say anything about Bible translations, let alone a specific English translation from the 1600s. Nor does the Bible identify which of the major text types is most reliable. The entire structure of the King James Only view thus rests on two crucial arguments. The first argument is that the idea of a perfect copy of the Bible is grounded in scripture. The Bible promises that God's word will stand forever (Isaiah 40:8), that not a single iota (or "jot") will pass from the law (Matthew 5:18), and that Jesus' words will never pass away (Matthew 24:35). In the King James Version, Psalm 12:6-7 declares that God will preserve his words forever. If there is no perfect Bible translation, then these promises have not been fulfilled. The second argument is that modern translations of the Bible are based on corrupt manuscripts, whereas the King James Version is based on a superior textual tradition, and reasons are given to support this conclusion.

The first argument is obviously overstated. For one thing, the King James translation of Psalm 12:6-7 is thought by most scholars to contain a translation error. Where it says, "Thou shalt keep them . . . thou shalt preserve them," scholars are almost unanimous in saying that "them" should be translated as "us." The context and grammar indicate that the author is speaking about people, not words.[29] If this is correct, then not only does the King James Bible contain translation errors, but one of its main prooftexts turns out to be completely misunderstood. (Other translation errors have been identified in the King James text as well.[30]) At the very least, the King James translation cannot be taken for granted.

Regardless of which translation we use, none of these prooftexts has the impact that King James Only proponents think they do. Suppose these verses do indicate that the written words of scripture will be perfectly preserved. Even in that case, we would still need some reason to connect this promise specifically to the King James Bible, otherwise we would simply be begging the question. Saying that God preserved his words perfectly is not the same as saying that God preserved his words perfectly *in one particular translation*. To extrapolate that meaning from the text, one already has to assume a King James Only perspective. But in that case, the prooftexts have no evidential value in this specific debate. As a result, all the weight of the King James Only movement rests on its assumptions about modern biblical scholarship. Are these assumptions justified?

The virtual consensus of biblical scholars is that the King James Version and the manuscript tradition it represents do not perfectly preserve the Bible's text. This includes almost every Christian Bible scholar in the world. That such a consensus exists in the world of academia, particularly Christian academia, is reflected in the sheer hostility that some proponents of the King James Only view feel toward Christian seminaries and most other institutions of higher learning.[31] In that case, the way we interpret certain Bible verses is irrelevant to the King James Only debate, since our interpretation is based on what side of the debate we land on. The question that really matters here is what we should do with scholarly testimony. Should we take it seriously or toss it aside?

At this point it is worth reflecting on what role a scholarly consensus should play in a discussion like this. We should probably never expect a perfect consensus on anything since, as Michael Licona says, "there will always be those who make their abode on the fringe."[32] Fringe ideas would include things like the flat-earth theory and the claim that vaccines cause autism.

There are certainly fringe views in the world of New Testament scholarship. There are a few (literally just a few) scholars with relevant credentials who continue to deny that Jesus existed, in spite of the many historical problems this creates, and contrary to the claims of just about every other scholar in the world.[33] Again, a few scholars have argued that the *Gospel of Peter* (a second-century writing possibly preserved in a seventh-century fragment) draws from an earlier narrative that was used by the authors of the Gospels in the New Testament when constructing their accounts of Jesus' final hours.[34] But the vast majority of scholars reject this theory in light of the sheer amount of special pleading that it requires.[35] Given the fact that fringe views like these exist, it is doubtful that a perfect consensus on important matters will ever be possible.

We should also be wary of a consensus that is formed by "stacking the deck," as was famously the case with the Jesus Seminar. This was a group of biblical scholars who voted using colored beads to determine which of Jesus' deeds or sayings were authentic. They presented their conclusions to the public as representative of scholarly opinion, but this was not entirely true since the group restricted its membership to scholars who tended to take more radical views about Jesus and the Bible. Their own internal consensus was hardly reflective of biblical scholarship in general, for which they were heavily criticized.[36]

For a consensus to be useful, something more is needed. Licona says:

> A group exhibiting greater heterogeneity [than the Jesus Seminar] is the Society of Biblical Literature (SBL). Annual SBL meetings are attended by members of many theological and philosophical persuasions: liberals, conservatives, Christians, Muslims, Hindus, Buddhists, agnostics and atheists, all from numerous countries and ethnic groups from all over the world. If a consensus opinion is going to be of any value for historians, it must come from such a group.[37]

Some proponents of the King James Only view regard the consensus of a mixed group like this as "anarchy," because they all hold conflicting views and therefore cannot collectively uphold the truth.[38] But this misses the point. The value of a consensus is not that it establishes the truth of everything every member in the group believes, nor even that it establishes the truth of whatever they all happen to agree on. Rather, the consensus reveals that the evidence for a certain position on a specific topic (say, the historical existence of Jesus) is so strong that the position commends itself to almost every trained scholar who studies it, even those who would be ideologically predisposed to deny such a thing.

This is why the consensus of scholarship is an important consideration for a topic like this. It is perfectly possible for a majority opinion to be mistaken, but if the majority consists of nearly every scholar on the planet who specializes in that field, regardless of their background, then an enormous burden of proof lies on the shoulders of those who would dismiss their claims so easily.

To be a King James Only Christian, you have to believe that the vast majority of biblical and textual scholars are either hopelessly incompetent or willfully part of an elaborate conspiracy to censor the true text of the Bible. This also applies to the majority of Christian scholars, including conservative evangelical scholars, including those who believe in the Bible's inerrancy. Their scholarship cannot be trusted because it merely represents the so-called wisdom of sinful human beings, whereas the King James Only view represents the wisdom of God.

The problem is obvious at this point. If human wisdom cannot be trusted, what does this mean for the King James Only movement itself? Where does the King James Only view come from, since it is not taught directly in the Bible? Obviously, it comes from certain Christian leaders who decided, in their wisdom, that the prevailing scholarship ought to be rejected. One defender of the King James

Only view even scoffs at the project of textual criticism, dismissing it as "some man's opinion who gave his preferences after considering some other men's opinions."[39] But is he not giving his own opinion after considering other people's opinions? What makes the wisdom of King James Only Christians more trustworthy than that of virtually the entire scholarly community? What makes their considered opinions on the matter more valuable than the scholarly opinions that they reject outright? Why should their wisdom be considered reliable, if they are sinful human beings as well? The answer cannot just be that they are "Bible-believing" Christians, because their interpretation of the Bible is rejected even by the vast majority of conservative Christian scholars. That means that the King James Only view needs to be justified on the basis of textual evidence.

However, by discrediting the scholarship of textual criticism, as King James Only Christians often do,[40] they make it impossible to assert that some manuscripts or text types are superior to others. After all, in order to make that determination, they need to know about the history of the manuscripts and the different text types, and they also need to know how to handle the textual variants—in other words, they need to engage in the very discipline that they have already dismissed. By calling human wisdom into question and rejecting the principles of textual criticism along with many other historical disciplines, the King James Only movement destroys its own foundation.

Additionally, the idea that the King James Version is both a perfect translation and the only reliable Bible translation is subject to several ironies. For starters, the translation has gone through a series of revisions since it was first published in 1611. The version known to most people today is based primarily on a revision from 1769. One function of these revisions was to correct errors in earlier editions.[41]

Furthermore, when the original edition was first published, it contained a preface written by the translators as well as marginal notes with alternate readings and explanations for difficulties in the text. In the preface, the translators defend the value of a translation that people can understand (bear in mind the preface was written in older English, and the spelling has not been updated):

> Happie is the man that delighteth in the Scripture, and thrise happie that meditateth in it day and night. But how shall men meditate in that, which they cannot understand? How shall they understand that which is kept close in an unknowen tongue?[42]

The translators seem to be unsympathetic to the idea of keeping the Bible frozen in an obscure rendering that most people cannot understand. They also make an interesting comment regarding imperfect Bible translations:

> Now to the later we answere; that wee doe not deny, nay wee affirme and avow, that the very meanest translation of the Bible in English, set foorth by men of our profession (for wee have seene none of theirs of the whole Bible as yet) containeth the word of God, nay, is the word of God. . . . No cause therefore why the word translated should bee denied to be the word, or forbidden to be currant, notwithstanding that some imperfections and blemishes may be noted in the setting foorth of it.[43]

For the King James translators, even if a Bible translation contains some errors, it should still be regarded as the Word of God.

Certain proponents of the King James Only view have argued that it does not matter what the translators themselves believed; it only matters what they produced. After all, King David did some terrible things in the Bible, yet we should still accept the psalms that (according to tradition) he wrote.[44] But when someone upholds a translation as perfect in spite of the claims of nearly every scholar in the world as well as the people who originally produced it, and if they do this on the basis of an opinion that relies on a discipline that they themselves have denounced, it is pretty clear that they have lost the thread.

The King James Only view turns out to be very similar to the kind of historical skepticism we discussed at the beginning of the chapter. Its proponents reject just about every claim made by trained specialists in any field pertaining to historical study, at least when it comes to the Bible. There is no amount of evidence that could possibly overturn their position on these matters. They have decided in advance, on other grounds, that historical knowledge cannot be built on such evidence. But just as radical skepticism defeats its own claims, the King James Only proponents, having cast all historical knowledge into doubt, then ask you to accept a specific set of historical claims on the testimony of a few people who have no grounds for making them, precisely because they have already destroyed those grounds themselves.

In light of these problems, the King James Only view should be laid to rest. This leaves us with the much more widely embraced version of biblical inerrancy, which attributes inspiration and inerrancy to the original writings but not to the copies which survive today and certainly not to any particular English translation, modern or otherwise. Even though we may find mistakes in the copies, the original biblical writings were completely free of errors and contradictions. We will see later that this formulation of the doctrine creates its own set of problems. However, before we can discuss that, we must consider the different ways that evangelicals apply the concept of inerrancy to the Bible.

Chapter Three

How Do Evangelicals Approach Inerrancy?

In the fall of 1978, a large gathering of prominent evangelical leaders met in Chicago to counter what they saw as a disturbing trend in the Christian world of subverting the divine authority of the Bible. Among those in attendance were some of the most influential evangelical leaders of the late twentieth century, including Norman Geisler, R. C. Sproul, John Warwick Montgomery, Carl F. H. Henry, Francis Schaeffer, and J. I. Packer. They drafted a statement articulating their commitment to biblical inerrancy, which became known as the Chicago Statement on Biblical Inerrancy (hereafter referred to as "CSBI"). Out of the two hundred and sixty-eight who were gathered, two hundred and forty voted to approve the statement.[1] The CSBI can still be easily accessed online.[2]

Certain excerpts from the statement are worth noting, especially since some of them will later prove to be quite troublesome for the doctrine:

We affirm that inspiration, strictly speaking, applies only to the autographic text of Scripture, which in the providence of God can be ascertained from available manuscripts with great accuracy. We further affirm that copies and translations of Scripture are the Word of God to the extent that they faithfully represent the original. (Article X)

We deny that it is proper to evaluate Scripture according to standards of truth and error that are alien to its usage or purpose. We further deny that inerrancy is negated by Biblical phenomena such as a lack of modern technical precision, irregularities of grammar or spelling, observational descriptions of nature, the reporting of falsehoods, the use of hyperbole and round numbers, the topical arrangement of material, variant selections of material in parallel accounts, or the use of free citations. (Article XIII)

We affirm that the doctrine of inerrancy is grounded in the teaching of the Bible about inspiration. We deny that Jesus' teaching about Scripture may be dismissed by appeals to accommodation or to any natural limitation of His humanity. (Article XV)

We affirm that the doctrine of inerrancy has been integral to the Church's faith throughout its history. We deny that inerrancy is a doctrine invented by Scholastic Protestantism, or is a reactionary position postulated in response to negative higher criticism. (Article XVI)

With these articles one begins to get a sense that the doctrine of inerrancy is not as straightforward as it initially seems. It appears that there are numerous qualifications that need to be kept in mind when deciding whether a verse in the Bible contains an error. What we would normally consider to be an error may not be counted as an error by those who believe in inerrancy.

In 2006, the Evangelical Theological Society decided to accept the CSBI as their official definition of the doctrine. The decision did not go over well with everyone in the evangelical community.[3] In fact, there has never been a consensus about how the doctrine of inerrancy should be understood, which is why certain evangelicals protest against making something like the CSBI normative for all who affirm the Bible's inerrancy.

A Spectrum of Opinions

It will help to lay out some of the different approaches that Christians take to the concept of inerrancy. We can do this by distinguishing more conservative approaches from more liberal ones. In the context of this discussion, the terminology has nothing to do with politics or social issues. Rather, it refers to how much flexibility one allows when acknowledging the impact of the human authors' perspectives or personalities on the text of the Bible. Within this framework, to go further in denying human influence on scripture is to move in a conservative direction, while going further in acknowledging human influence is to move in a liberal direction.

At one end of the inerrancy spectrum, which we can call the extreme conservative end, we have the so-called "dictation theory" which holds that the human authors of scripture were basically God's secretaries. God gave them the exact words, and they simply recorded them. This is as literal a view of inspiration as one can have.

Since God chose the words, human influence on the text is basically nonexistent. In spite of the fact that some Bible passages can easily be read this way (like when Jesus dictates seven letters to John in the book of Revelation), the dictation view is widely rejected for the simple reason that the authors of the Bible have different vocabularies and distinct writing styles, a clear indication that human creativity played some role in the writing of the Bible.[4]

At the more liberal end of the spectrum are those who seem to regard biblical teachings as indispensable but do not commit to a clear affirmation or denial of inerrancy, people like N. T. Wright and Craig Evans. Both are highly influential, widely respected biblical scholars who consciously reject fundamentalism while identifying as evangelicals. However, their precise views on the Bible's accuracy and internal consistency can be difficult to pin down.

Evans regards it as a mistake to place one's faith in "believing that the Scriptures must be inerrant according to rather idiosyncratic standards" or in believing that "we must be able to harmonize the four Gospels."[5] He is comfortable regarding certain passages in the Gospels as being more reflective of "ecclesiastical proclivities" than factual historical reporting.[6] Evans is also willing to say that in Mark 2:26, where Jesus names the wrong high priest when recalling a story about King David, "we have a mistake, technically speaking, either made by Jesus himself or by Mark (or perhaps by someone who passed on the story)."[7] Yet at no point (at least none that I am aware of) does he explicitly deny inerrancy, and his writing sometimes appears in resources which take a stricter approach to the Bible than he does. His exposition of the Bible's meaning is perfectly in line with the views of his more conservative colleagues.[8]

As for Wright, he opts out of labeling himself an inerrantist because for him that term reflects a modern rationalist and fundamentalist context which misses the point of what the Bible is talking about.[9] He is comfortable admitting that the four Gospel accounts of Jesus' resurrection "do not fit snugly together," although he falls short of saying they contradict each other.[10] He says that he is "not unhappy with what people are trying to affirm when they use words like 'infallible' (the idea that the Bible won't deceive us) and 'inerrant' (the stronger idea, that the Bible can't get things wrong)" though he avoids those terms himself.[11]

I can certainly understand some of these sentiments, especially since I would agree that inerrancy is a modern doctrine, but I must confess that the hesitation to make a clear affirmation or denial of inerrancy, and to explore the ramifications of that choice, seems odd to me. I also do not see the difference between a mistake and "a mistake, technically speaking." Presumably a mistake in the Bible, technical or not, means that the Bible is not inerrant, at least not in the unlimited sense.

Wright suggests that debates over inerrancy "distract attention from the real point of what the Bible is there for,"[12] and he is not alone in this assessment, but this seems to dodge an important question. Certainly it makes a big difference whether or not the Bible gets anything wrong. If nothing else, it raises questions about how the Bible can be a divine revelation. Do Wright and Evans think that Christians are allowed to reject the truth of certain biblical ideas or narratives? If not, then why not? And if so, then how much can a Christian reject?

People like Evans and Wright want their readers to accept biblical teachings about a number of issues. In that case, it seems all the more important to provide a rigorous justification for *why* humans are obligated to accept the things that the Bible affirms or teaches. Inerrancy may be a doctrine developed in the shadow of an outdated modernist philosophy, but it clearly aims to affirm something that Christians have been talking about ever since the church came into existence.

Most Christians who believe in the Bible's inerrancy probably fall somewhere in between these two ends of the spectrum, rejecting the extremes of dictation theory on the one hand and ambiguous non-committal on the other. They mostly seem to agree that the Bible contains God's words, although these words were written by particular people in particular contexts. But beyond the main areas of agreement, there are plenty of in-house debates.

Areas of Disagreement

Inerrantists disagree strongly with each other about when it is appropriate to interpret the Bible metaphorically instead of literally. Michael Licona, a conservative believer in inerrancy,[13] found himself mired in controversy after a comment, buried in a massive historical defense of Jesus' resurrection, regarding the meaning of two strange verses in the New Testament. These verses report an unusual event at the time of Jesus' death:

> The tombs also were opened, and many bodies of the saints who had fallen asleep[14] were raised. After his resurrection they came out of the tombs and entered the holy city and appeared to many. (Matthew 27:52-53)

The difficulty with a literal interpretation of this passage is that the resurrection of "many" holy people who entered Jerusalem and "appeared to many" would have been an event of enormous significance to the early church, yet nobody else in the ancient Christian world seems to know of this event apart from references to the passage in Matthew. It gets no mention in the other Gospels, the letters of Paul, the book of Acts, or any other New Testament writing, to say nothing of non-Christian sources like the writings of Josephus. If such an event really took place—that is, if "many" resurrected saints really had revealed themselves to "many" witnesses in the city where Christianity began—it is hard to understand why it got so little attention.[15]

Licona also observes the oddity of the author's comment that the resurrected saints came to life at the time of Jesus' death but did not come out of their tombs until after Jesus' resurrection, given the fact that Jesus died on a Friday and rose on a Sunday. He asks, "What were they doing between Friday afternoon and early Sunday morning? Were they standing in the now open doorways of their tombs and waiting?"[16] Licona does not believe that these verses are wrong. Instead, he concludes that the author is using a poetic device, sort of like "special effects" which are meant to enhance the narrative.[17]

For this comment, Licona was publicly denounced by a number of evangelical leaders.[18] He was particularly targeted by Norman Geisler, one of the scholars behind the CSBI.[19] But the strange thing about this controversy is that Licona was not saying anything new. He was restating a point that had already been made by other evangelical scholars. William Lane Craig, one of the most celebrated apologists in the evangelical world, argued long before Licona published his book that the author of Matthew did not intend the story of the resurrected saints to be taken literally. In fact, he notes that "probably only a few conservative scholars would treat the story as historical."[20]

Another area where inerrantists can disagree quite strongly is on how much variance between the four Gospels can be granted without admitting any contradictions. Some assume that if there is any difference between two biblical accounts of the same event, the best approach is to treat them as separate events. Even though the Gospels may agree with each other that Peter denied Jesus three times, the differences between the accounts mean that he really must have denied Jesus six times,[21] and even though the Gospels each only report that Jesus caused a disturbance in the Jewish temple once, the fact that they place the event at different points in Jesus' ministry means that he must have done this twice.[22]

Others are less credulous toward this sort of harmonization, and far more willing to allow for a significant amount of variation between the Gospels, due to the effects that oral transmission and ancient writing standards would have had on storytelling in the ancient world. On this view, such differences are not against the rules for ancient writers and thus do not count as true errors or contradictions.[23] Thus, if one Gospel says that a centurion approached Jesus directly (Matthew 8:5-6), and another Gospel says that the centurion sent Jewish elders to speak to Jesus on his behalf (Luke 7:2-3), this is not necessarily a contradiction. Details like that would (allegedly) not matter in an ancient context, and that is the only context by which it is fair to judge an ancient writing.[24]

One further area of disagreement worth mentioning is the question of whether Genesis is best interpreted through the lens of creationism, Intelligent Design, or Darwinism. Many conservative Christians believe that the Bible requires a literal interpretation of the creation narratives.[25] Some inerrantists opt instead for a theory of Intelligent Design. The main thrust of this theory is the claim that biological complexity is best explained by design rather than natural selection. Intelligent Design does not require a particular reading of Genesis. In fact, it allows for an old earth, biological evolution, and the reality of death prior to the existence of human beings.[26] Finally, there are some inerrantists who affirm biblical inerrancy while passionately defending a Darwinian view of human origins.[27]

Since there is no "one size fits all" version of the doctrine of inerrancy, it follows that there is no consensus regarding what it would mean for the doctrine to be false. For some who affirm the doctrine, if humans evolved by natural selection, or if the four Gospels cannot be perfectly harmonized in a strictly literal fashion, then biblical inerrancy is a joke. For others, none of this would do anything to overturn the authority or inerrancy of scripture. Different Christians appeal to the same texts, but they see them in quite different ways. This makes it a bit more difficult to assess the credibility of the doctrine.

What Inerrancy Looks Like in Practice

We can get a good sense of how complicated the inerrancy debate can be by looking at a couple of instances where the Bible seems to get something wrong, yet proving an error or falsehood is seemingly impossible. To begin with, the New Testament provides two different accounts of Judas Iscariot's death. Judas was one of Jesus' twelve disciples, best known for betraying him to the local authorities. According to Matthew 27:5, after being filled with remorse for playing a key role in Jesus' arrest, Judas goes somewhere (the location is not identified) and hangs himself. But according to Acts 1:18, after betraying Jesus, Judas acquires a field, and at some point he falls headlong (presumably in the field), then his body bursts open and his bowels gush out. (It should be noted that Acts never identifies Judas' death as a suicide.) We are obviously dealing with two different accounts of the same man's death, but "different" does not necessarily mean "incompatible." I am familiar with three theories Christians have offered to harmonize these stories.

The first theory is simple: Judas hanged himself on a branch over a cliff, and then at some point the branch broke, and his body fell to the ground and burst asunder. The second theory is similar, but makes no appeal to a cliff. Instead, it suggests that after Judas hanged himself in the field, his body swelled up (as opposed to "falling headlong"; apparently this is a translation issue). Eventually, the rope snapped or the branch broke, at which point the corpse fell to the ground and, due to its state of decomposition, burst open.[28]

Some Christians resolve the discrepancy differently, by appealing to a third theory which is less concerned with reading the Bible in a literalistic fashion. This theory suggests that only the account found in Acts gives us the actual, literal description of Judas' death: he fell headlong in a field and his body burst open. The author of Matthew, on the other hand, is employing a method of interpretation called "typology." This method treats a person or event in the Old Testament, referred to as a "type," as corresponding to something in the New Testament.[29] For instance, in Romans 5:14, Paul says that Adam is "a type of the one who was to come," namely, Jesus. Paul sees a correspondence between Adam's sin, resulting in death, and Jesus' obedience, resulting in life.

The argument we are considering suggests that by saying that Judas "went and hanged himself," the author of Matthew is not saying that Judas *literally* went and hanged himself. Rather, the phrasing is meant to echo an account in the Old Testament concerning a man named Ahithophel who conspired against King David. According to the story, upon realizing that events had not gone according to plan, Ahithophel went and hanged himself (2 Samuel 17:23). By echoing the story, Matthew is saying that Ahithophel is a type of Judas. When the author says that Judas hanged himself, what he really means is that Judas "died a death worthy of that traitor Ahithophel."[30]

One issue I see with a typological reading of Matthew's account is that it is not incompatible with the idea that Judas literally hanged himself. Even if we suppose that the author of Matthew saw a connection between Ahithophel and Judas, it is entirely possible that their similar manners of death were part of the reason that the author made this connection in the first place. Anyone can see a parallel between Ahithophel betraying David and hanging himself, and Judas betraying Jesus and hanging himself, but if the author of Matthew did not believe that Judas had actually hanged himself, then he had to notice the parallel on different grounds.

J. P. Holding and Nick Peters claim that the author of Matthew is telling us that "Judas fulfilled the 'type' of Ahithophel by being a traitor who responded with grief and then died."[31] The problem here is that the story of Ahithophel never says anything at all about his grief or remorse. Holding and Peters are reading that detail into the story.

This means that, if Judas did not literally hang himself, then the author of Matthew would have had to connect Judas' death to the story of Ahithophel purely on the basis that they were both traitors who died. It seems just as easy to believe that the author of Matthew really thought Judas had hanged himself and simply reported the event. Thus, even if we could prove that the account in Matthew is meant to be understood typologically, that would not be enough to demonstrate that he was not trying to give a literal description of Judas' death.

In spite of all this, it is worth noting that this typological reading of Matthew is not just an odd theory promulgated by fundamentalists. In fact, this is not a fundamentalist interpretation at all, since fundamentalists would insist on reading the story in Matthew more literally. The possibility that Matthew's account has some relationship to the story of Ahithophel is a serious point of discussion in the scholarly world, even if it is not widely embraced.[32]

We have now seen three different ways of harmonizing the different accounts of Judas' death. Even if we do not find any of these theories to be persuasive, it would be difficult to prove that the two accounts actually contradict each other on this point. Maybe they do, but they do not offer compelling evidence against the doctrine of inerrancy for those who already believe it.

Next, we turn to the genealogy of Jesus—or rather, "genealogies," since there are two given in the New Testament. One is found in Matthew 1:1-16, and the other is found in Luke 3:23-28. According to both Gospels, Jesus' parents were Mary and Joseph. Matthew traces Jesus' ancestry through Joseph back to Abraham, whereas Luke traces it all the way back to "Adam, son of God."

To say that the genealogies are different is an understatement. There is no question that these are not the same genealogy. They do not even agree on the name of Jesus' grandfather. In Matthew, it is Jacob; in Luke, it is Heli. They also identify Jesus as a descendent of King David through different lines. Matthew follows the line of David's son Solomon, while Luke follows the line of a different son Nathan. Predictably, many of the names in the two genealogies do not match up.

In addition to this discrepancy between the two Gospels, several elements of Matthew's genealogy might seem clearly erroneous to a modern reader. For instance, the author divides the genealogy into three groups, and sums them up by saying, "So all the generations from Abraham to David are fourteen generations; and from David to the deportation to Babylon, fourteen generations; and from the deportation to Babylon to the Messiah, fourteen generations" (Matthew 1:17). Clearly, the number fourteen has some kind of significance for the author, possibly because fourteen is the numerical value of David's name in Hebrew.[33] However, the claim that each segment of Matthew's genealogy contains fourteen generations is artificial. Three groups of fourteen would add up to forty-two, but Matthew's list only contains forty-one names total. It seems that the author is counting someone twice.

When we compare Matthew's genealogy to the records found in 1 Chronicles, we can also see that Matthew's version omits quite a few names. Furthermore, the author seems to make a mistake when he lists Zerubbabel as the son of Shealtiel. (For clarity, the Greek transliteration of Shealtiel is "Salathiel" which is why the name appears that way in some translations.) This conflicts with 1 Chronicles 2:16-19, which identifies Zerubbabel as the son of Pediah, Shealtiel's brother. One might think, in light of all this, that the genealogies of Jesus provide a clear refutation of biblical inerrancy—but as we will see shortly, things are far more complicated than they appear.

The fact that Matthew and Luke present two different genealogies has been a point of discussion since the days of early Christianity. Writing in the fourth century CE, Eusebius acknowledges that many people viewed it as a contradiction. He puts forward the theory that Joseph's natural father was Jacob (thus the genealogy of Matthew) and that after Jacob died, Joseph's mother married Heli, who became Joseph's legal father (thus the genealogy of Luke).[34] Here we can see that Eusebius is appealing to the same law of levirate marriage we encountered earlier when discussing Jesus and the Sadducees. Some apologetics resources still use Eusebius' argument.[35] Other apologists prefer the theory that Matthew records Jesus' lineage through Joseph whereas Luke records Jesus' lineage through Mary.[36]

From a historical perspective—that is, a perspective that makes no appeal to Christian theology—we have absolutely no way to know if either of these genealogies is accurate (how could we?), and there is no reason to assume that they *must* be accurate apart from a theological commitment to a particular view of the Bible. Raymond Brown has offered a persuasive argument against the explanation promoted by Eusebius, which he concludes by saying, "The theory of a levirate marriage solves so little and has so many difficulties that it should be abandoned as a solution in the problem of the two genealogies, and even in the more restricted problem of Jesus' overabundance of grandfathers."[37] As for the other theory, that Luke preserves the lineage of Mary, it is sheer speculation. Nevertheless, it cannot be disproven.

There is some question over whether the author of Matthew intentionally omitted certain names or whether he was working from a source in which the names were already omitted.[38] If it stems from the source material, we might think that this counts as a (quite understandable and unintentional) error on the author's part, since he was just copying the information he had available—except that the exact same point is used by some apologists to defend Matthew's accuracy.[39] Even if the author did intentionally omit certain names, apologists deny that this is fraudulent activity on the grounds that he is engaging in a practice called "telescoping," which was allowable for ancient writers.[40]

Likewise, the contradiction regarding the father of Zerubbabel is not necessarily a falsehood, strange as it sounds. Even non-evangelical resources consider the possibility that Shealtiel died without having any children, at which point his brother Pedaiah stepped in to fulfill the legal requirement to provide offspring for his brother's widow (levirate marriage again!).[41] This is precisely the explanation used by the apologists, although there is some disagreement about whether Pedaiah sired Shealtiel's children, or the other way around.[42]

Skeptics of inerrancy may say that there is no reason to think the genealogies are either compatible or accurate, and then perhaps assume as a default position, given the laxity of ancient history standards, that they probably are not. Inerrantists will assume, as a matter of doctrine, that both genealogies are correct. The end result is a stalemate. And while I fall into the skeptical group myself, I personally have no objection to the possibility that some of the apologists' theories may in fact be correct.

What bothers me more is the way that certain "inerrancy deniers" will still appeal to the genealogies as if they present a clear, decisive proof that the Bible contradicts itself. Bart Ehrman does this in one of his books, declaring without any further discussion that neither genealogy presents Mary's lineage, because both genealogies mention Joseph instead of Mary.[43] I do not think Ehrman is necessarily wrong, but in a debate over biblical inerrancy, who is this declaration meant to persuade? It certainly will not persuade those who believe in inerrancy, because they already know about this issue and have a theory to explain it, and it would be hard to prove them wrong. So this particular issue, while interesting, does not really move the debate anywhere.

Because biblical inerrancy is a flexible concept in theory, and a slippery concept in practice, deciding what it means for the doctrine to be true or false can be quite difficult. The challenge for the skeptic of inerrancy is to produce compelling counter-evidence which cannot be avoided by any version of the doctrine. Of course, this assumes that the truth of the matter really can be settled by evidence. We will see later that many inerrantists rule this possibility out in advance. But before we can talk about that, we need to dig a bit further into the way that defenders of inerrancy interpret the Bible.

Chapter Four

How Do Inerrantists
Interpret the Bible?

Back in my fundamentalist days I sometimes encountered people who argued that they did not need to rely on anyone's interpretation of the Bible. Instead, they claimed that they were just sticking with what the Bible plainly says. This is obviously based on a simple misunderstanding. To talk about what the Bible "plainly says" implies that the meaning of the Bible is clear for anyone who reads it, but to have an opinion about what the Bible means requires interpretation to some degree. Interpretation is just another word for "explaining the meaning of." Unless we are prepared to deny that the Bible has any meaning, it would be impossible to understand the Bible without interpreting it.

Even when we read a book silently while we are alone, our minds are busy at work interpreting the words, because that is the only way for us to understand the text's meaning. If our minds did not do this, then the text would appear to us as a bunch of meaningless symbols, the way it does to children before they learn how to read. Assuming that we are all literate, it follows that we all engage in the practice of interpreting texts to some extent, whether we realize it or not. You are doing it at this very moment. (If you are not literate, I commend you on making it this far into the book.)

Since we cannot understand a text without interpreting it, there is an obvious benefit to putting careful thought into how we form our interpretations. The discipline which aims to identify the correct principles of interpretation is called "hermeneutics." There are different theories of hermeneutics at play when it comes to interpreting the Bible, so it is important to identify some of these theories before we attempt to draw any conclusions based on the Bible's content.

Historical Criticism

A large portion of the Bible consists of historical narratives, and one of the defining features of both Judaism and Christianity is the belief that God has acted within human history. It is no surprise that historical concerns feature prominently in discussions about the Bible. Scholars, Christian or otherwise, frequently use what is called the "historical-critical method." The word "critical," in this context, has nothing to do with ridiculing anything. Rather, it has to do with applying careful thought to certain questions or problems.[1] The historical-critical method involves a handful of related disciplines aimed at answering the historical questions that come up when reading the Bible.[2] One of these disciplines is textual criticism, which we encountered earlier and which aims to establish the authentic text. The other disciplines look for the meaning of the text by analyzing its written sources, discerning the forms of the oral traditions that lie behind some of the written material, and considering how the authors or editors used their sources and put the texts into their final form.[3]

The point of historical criticism is to get at the meaning of a text by seeing how it would have been understood in its original context. Part of this process involves asking questions about the author's intention. What was the author trying to say? It might seem surprising, but this notion of "authorial intent" is somewhat controversial. We will come back to this topic later.

One reason why historical criticism of the Bible makes some Christians feel nervous is that it seeks to answer these historical questions without depending on the authority of the church or its traditions. It does not assume, from the outset, that traditional Christian interpretations of the Bible are correct. The goal for historical critics is to try to let the evidence speak for itself.

It is easy to see why proponents of inerrancy might take issue with the way that historical critics approach the Bible. Thus, we find these words in the CSBI:

> We affirm that the text of Scripture is to be interpreted by grammatico-historical exegesis, taking account of its literary forms and devices, and that Scripture is to interpret Scripture. We deny the legitimacy of any treatment of the text or quest for sources lying behind it that leads to relativizing, dehistoricizing, or discounting its teaching, or rejecting its claims to authorship. (Article XVIII)

The signers of the CSBI claim that the Bible must be interpreted by what they call "grammatico-historical exegesis." The word "exegesis" refers to carefully interpreting a text based on its content. (The opposite would be "eisegesis," which interprets a text based on reading things into it. This is generally something that interpreters try to avoid.) The term "grammatico-historical" is a bit confusing, since it seems to be a distinctly Christian method of studying the Bible.

At first glance, the grammatico-historical method sounds very similar to the historical-critical method. Based on the statement quoted above, it consists of trying to discern the correct meaning of a biblical text by carefully studying its "literary forms and devices." The key difference lies in denying "the legitimacy of any treatment of the text or quest for sources lying behind it that leads to relativizing, dehistoricizing, or discounting its teaching, or rejecting its claims to authorship." Whereas historical criticism sets out to follow the evidence wherever it leads, grammatico-historical exegesis already has an idea of where the evidence should take us. If it doesn't take us where we want to go, then we need to go back and try again. This method assumes in advance that the "real" meaning of the text is always true, and that it will conform with the church's theological views. Obviously, historians in general do not make this assumption when studying historical texts, and most biblical scholars do not impose this rule on themselves when studying the Bible.

Another principle the CSBI insists on, which no modern scholar outside the evangelical world would consider binding, is the rule that "Scripture is to interpret Scripture." This means that any passage of the Bible may be found to shed light on the meaning of a different passage, even if they were written at different times in completely different contexts. We encountered this strategy earlier when we talked about how Jews and Christians in the ancient world interpreted their scriptures. It is a natural corollary of the assumption that all scripture ultimately comes from the same divine author.

Traditionalists And Contextualists

Sometimes conservative Christians are described as people who interpret the Bible "literally," but this can be misleading since, in plenty of cases, even a staunch literalist can recognize a metaphor. For instance, not many inerrantists would read Hebrews 12:29 and conclude that God is a literal flame of fire. To call God a "consuming fire" is to speak metaphorically. When Jesus tells the story of the prodigal son, inerrantists usually recognize that he is telling a parable, not recounting some event that really happened. (Also, it's perfectly possible for someone to interpret a Bible passage literally without believing that what it says is true. In that sense, "literalists" need not be Christian.)

Inerrantists usually shy away from interpreting the biblical text in a heavily symbolic way unless the context demands it, as with a book like Revelation, which is full of vivid imagery that often defies literal interpretation. Generally speaking, their goal is not necessarily to interpret the Bible with absolute literalism across the board, but rather to accept the meaning which was intended by the person who wrote the text.

Inerrantists do not all agree on precisely how to determine the meaning of a text, as we saw earlier when we discussed the controversy surrounding Michael Licona's interpretation of Matthew 27:52-53. This passage describes the resurrection of a number of holy people who entered Jerusalem and appeared to many witnesses. Licona suggests that the best way to understand the text is as an elaborate poetic device to emphasize the significance of Jesus' death. His critics insist that this is tantamount to rejecting the teaching of scripture. In this way, we can see two very different approaches to interpreting the Bible taken by inerrantists.[4]

One could be called the "traditionalist" approach, as represented by people like Norman Geisler and others who participated in writing the CSBI. This approach leans much more heavily into interpreting the Bible as literally as possible. The traditionalist reading of the passage from Matthew entails that a number of people were literally raised from the dead at the time of Jesus' death, and that they literally appeared to witnesses in the city a few days later. Since Matthew is a Gospel, and since Gospels are biographical accounts, then the narratives found within the Gospel should be understood as reporting actual events.

The other approach could be called the "contextualist" approach, which embraces inerrancy but does not commit itself in principle to interpreting a narrative literally if the context demands otherwise. It also seeks to avoid imposing a modern Western understanding of what it means for a text to be in error. Licona's reading of the passage from Matthew falls into this category, although the contextualist approach does not rule out more literal interpretations altogether. It is true that the Gospels are similar to a form of Greco-Roman biography called *bios*,[5] but ancient biographies were not written according to the same rules that modern biographies are. Ancient authors could employ a surprising amount of creativity in how they presented their material. Licona writes, "Because *bios* was a flexible genre, it is often difficult to determine where history ends and legend begins."[6]

To get a good sense of how different these approaches are, we can consider the Old Testament books of Esther and Jonah. Most modern scholars see these books as non-historical narratives on the grounds that *this is how they are supposed to be understood.* Jonah functions as a satire and Esther is an ancient Jewish novella.[7] This idea is quite compatible with a contextualist view of inerrancy. To look through these books for historical errors would thus be somewhat irrelevant. Equally irrelevant would be the common complaint from skeptical readers about the credibility of Jonah surviving for three days in the belly of a giant fish. By contrast, on a traditionalist view of inerrancy, Jonah and Esther are historical narratives, and that is the end of the discussion. The events they record really happened exactly as described, otherwise the Bible is not inerrant.

Traditionalists almost assume that if the Bible presents a narrative, then it was intended to be taken literally unless you can prove otherwise. Contextualists deny that the meaning of biblical narratives must always be literal, and are willing to be quite flexible in what they accept as the probable intended meaning by the author. In spite of these important differences, we can see that both groups are operating under the assumption that the meaning of a text lies in how it was intended to be understood in its original context.

Allegorical Interpretation

The emphasis on the original intended meaning is a common theme in discussions about inerrancy. However, ancient Christian theologians did not limit themselves to sticking with the meaning of the text in its original historical context. David R. Law explains, "The dominant method of biblical exegesis in the early Church was *allegorical interpretation*."[8] Allegorical readings of scripture looked beyond the literal meaning of the text in order to get to a hidden meaning.[9] By interpreting a text as an allegory, ancient interpreters would imbue the details of a narrative with deep symbolic significance.

Augustine had a fondness for extravagant allegorical biblical interpretations that went well beyond what we would regard as the text's actual meaning. For example he believed that Jesus' parable of the Good Samaritan (found in Luke 10:25-37) was full of hidden symbols. On his reading, the man in the story represents Adam and the human race, the city of Jerusalem is "heavenly peace," the city of Jericho is our mortality, the thieves are the devil and his angels, the stolen goods are human immortality, the priest and the Levite are the priesthood and ministry of the Old Testament, the Samaritan is Jesus, the Samaritan's horse is Jesus' human flesh, the bandages are "the containment of sins," the inn is the church, the innkeeper is the apostle Paul, and so on.[10]

This is far removed from the probable intended meaning of the story, which is framed as Jesus' response to a question about what it means to love your neighbor. Jesus is certainly not trying to say anything about Paul and Adam. As Marcus Borg points out, "For Jesus, it is a story of what it means to be compassionate."[11] But for Augustine, the meaning of scripture was not limited to what the original author intended. On the contrary, he was quite convinced that it was possible that there were true interpretations of biblical passages unknown even to the original human authors, which could be revealed by God to later readers.[12]

The early church's love for allegorical interpretations sheds clear light on why it is important to differentiate between the modern doctrine of inerrancy and ancient Christian beliefs regarding scripture's perfect truthfulness. As Law observes, "For the allegorical interpreter, the tensions, inconsistencies and contradictions in the text are signposts alerting the reader to a deeper level of spiritual meaning underlying the surface meaning of the text."[13] In other words, ancient authors were not oblivious toward errors or contradictions in their sacred scriptures, but since they believed that all scripture was inspired, they sometimes took these things as indications that the "real" meaning of the text must lie beyond a literal interpretation.

For ancient theologians, the literal sense of scripture was the plain, historical, non-symbolic meaning.[14] It was precisely because of the difficulties they faced when trying to interpret scripture literally that so many ancient Christians opted for non-literal interpretations. For example, in reference to the biblical stories about God commanding the Israelites to slaughter their enemies in the Promised Land, a Christian theologian named Origen wrote these words in the third century: "As for the command given to the Jews to slay their enemies, it may be answered that anyone who looks carefully into the meaning of the passage will find that it is impossible to interpret it literally."[15]

A more dramatic example comes in the writing of Gregory of Nyssa in the fourth century. Gregory's most significant contribution to Christian theology involves his work on the doctrine of the Trinity, which played an important role in the development of the standard Christian vocabulary about God as one substance and three persons.[16] In a work called *The Life of Moses*, Gregory discusses the story of the exodus and the ten plagues on Egypt. As part of that discussion, he talks about the final plague, in which God kills all the firstborn in Egypt (Exodus 12:29-32).

Gregory does not believe that the story concerns the literal killing of children, but rather it teaches us "that it is necessary to destroy utterly the first birth of evil." His reasons for taking this view are fascinating:

> It does not seem good to me to pass this interpretation by without further contemplation. How would a concept worthy of God be preserved in the description of what happened if one looked only to the history? The Egyptian acts unjustly, and in his place is punished his newborn child, who in his infancy cannot discern what is good and what is not. His life has no experience of evil, for infancy is not capable of passion. He does not know to distinguish between his right hand and his left. . . . If such a one now pays the penalty of his father's wickedness, where is justice? Where is piety? Where is holiness? Where is Ezekiel, who cries: *The man who has sinned is the man who must die and a son is not to suffer for the sins of his father?* How can the history so contradict reason?[17]

It is for this reason that Gregory looks for "the true spiritual meaning" of the story by interpreting it "typologically," a method of interpretation that we encountered earlier when discussing the suicide of Judas Iscariot.[18]

Gregory's belief that scripture cannot contradict itself, along with his belief that it could not depict God as unjust, moved him to reject the literal, historical meaning behind the exodus narrative. Such an interpretation, in his mind, could never be reconciled with the teaching of the prophet Ezekiel, who staunchly denies that children have to suffer for the sins of their parents (Ezekiel 18:4, 20). Modern critical scholars, whether evangelical or not, will almost certainly agree that Gregory's interpretation does not reflect the original intended meaning of the narrative in Exodus. But for Gregory, it is only by rejecting the historical meaning that the truth and coherence of scripture can be preserved.

This is a vastly different way of preserving the Bible's theological and moral integrity than what we find in modern evangelical Christianity. Consider Gleason Archer's response to this same passage. How can it be that God kills the firstborn child of every Egyptian family due to the stubbornness of its ruler? Archer answers, "There is no way for nations to be dealt with other than on a collective basis."[19] He accuses the general populace of Egypt of being too lazy to challenge their evil ruler: "Conceivably a coup d'etat might have toppled Pharaoh from his throne in time to avert this approaching catastrophe, but his subjects were content to let him make the fateful decision as their lawful ruler."[20] Geisler agrees, saying that "it is also wrong to assume that simply because the Egyptian people *did not* change Pharaoh's mind that they *could not* have changed his mind."[21] There is no hesitation to embrace the literal meaning here.

I will have more to say about these kinds of sentiments later,[22] but for now I just want to call attention to the problem with Article XVI of the CSBI: "We affirm that the doctrine of inerrancy has been integral to the Church's faith throughout its history." As we have seen, ancient theologians sometimes retained the integrity of the Bible by denying the interpretive strategies that modern inerrantists see as essential for the integrity of their doctrine. That is not an argument against inerrancy, but it does reveal that Christians who seek to harmonize their scriptures today and those who did so in ancient times are often treating the Bible in strikingly different ways. To say that the doctrine of inerrancy as presented in the CSBI has been integral to the church's faith is simply false.

Conflicting Commitments

Inerrantists who accept the CSBI are firmly committed to upholding the original intended meaning of the biblical texts, but they also claim that scripture must interpret scripture. So what happens when these two commitments come into conflict? What if scripture does not interpret scripture in a manner that is faithful to the original intent of the author?

Deuteronomy 25:4 says, "You shall not muzzle an ox while it is treading out the grain." This seems pretty straightforward. After all, there are plenty of laws in the Bible about the proper management of oxen (for example, in Exodus 21:28-36). There is no reason to think that the text means anything other than what it plainly says. However, ancient interpreters of scripture had a tendency to assume that everything written in the scriptures was meant to apply to their present circumstances.[23] The apostle Paul says of the stories in the Old Testament, "These things happened to them to serve as an example to us, and they were written down to instruct us" (1 Corinthians 10:11). Not surprisingly, Paul is able to find a contemporary meaning in the passage from Deuteronomy, and it has nothing to do with oxen.

After defending his status as an apostle, Paul mentions that he should have the right to earn a living from his apostolic ministry.

He justifies his view by appealing to the above-mentioned scripture passage:

> It is written in the law of Moses, "You shall not muzzle an ox while it is treading out the grain." Is it for oxen that God is concerned? Or does he not speak entirely for our sake? It was indeed written for our sake, for whoever plows should plow in hope and whoever threshes should thresh in hope of a share in the crop. (1 Corinthians 9:8-10)

Paul is not suggesting that the original passage has two meanings, one which applies to oxen, and the other which applies to apostles. Rather, he flatly denies that God is concerned about oxen, and suggests that the verse was written "entirely for our sake."

If we go by the original intended meaning, Deuteronomy 25:4 is talking about oxen, but according to Paul, it is not talking about oxen. These two meanings conflict with each other, yet those who accept the CSBI are committed in principle to affirming both. As a result, this version of inerrancy is literally self-defeating. Its methodology is impossible to apply consistently.

The Bible does not allow interpreters to restrict its meaning to the original intent of the authors. Presumably, biblical inerrancy requires an acceptance of Paul's interpretation of the passage about oxen. If the meaning of a text is limited to what the original author intended, then Paul's interpretation is wrong—the passage in Deuteronomy was not really written "entirely for our sake"—and it would seem that the Bible is not inerrant. So now we have to consider the hermeneutical question for ourselves. What is the best way to interpret a written text? How do we go about discerning its meaning? And can it have multiple layers of meaning?

Chapter Five

How Can We Determine a
Text's Meaning?

When I was in college, I took a course on biblical hermeneutics. Our textbook stated that "the Bible is true in all that it intends to teach."[1] I remember being struck by the oddness of this phrase, since it appeals to the intention of the Bible rather than the human authors. What could it mean for the Bible to intend anything? The Bible is not a sentient being. Wouldn't it would make more sense to speak of the authors' intentions?

The role of the author's intention in determining the meaning of the text is a somewhat controversial idea. There are several reasons for this. First, by focusing on the author's intention, the interpreter seems to favor the earliest form of the text, whereas many books in the Bible reached their final form through a process of editing (a point to which we shall return). One might think that the meaning of these final forms carries a significant amount of weight, since those are the versions that have been received by the church as scripture.[2] Second, and somewhat related, is the fact that some books in the Bible are widely thought to have been produced by a community rather than a single author. It would seem like a mistake in these cases to think that the meaning of the text is determined by the intention of a single person.[3] A third challenge comes from those who doubt that the author of a book has anything to do with its meaning at all. On their view, meaning in the text comes from the reader's encounter with it. Meaning is created, not discovered.

Some historical critics suggest that it is better to speak of the intention of the text rather than the intention of the author.[4] This could be why my college textbook spoke of the Bible's intention. I think I can understand the impulse here—it really does seem like there are different ways for a text to carry meaning—but I find this idea a little confusing for the reason I mentioned earlier. Intentions can only be attributed to persons, not to texts.

For the inerrantist, it might be tempting to say that "the Bible is true in all that God intends to teach through it." This correctly attributes intentionality to a person rather than a book, but it also raises a difficult question. Can God put meaning into a text that the original human author did not intend, as Augustine believed? This might seem like an attractive option, at least for the one who accepts biblical inerrancy, but it comes at a price, since the principles of historical criticism and even grammatico-historical exegesis would no longer apply.

If God inspires me to write something whose meaning eludes even me, then how can the meaning be determined by my historical or cultural context? God has no such context. In that case, it would not matter what kind of book I thought I was writing, or the audience I thought I was writing to. If the Bible's "real" meaning is determined by what God intends to say, and if God's message is potentially different from what the human authors thought they were writing, the end result is an interpretive free-for-all.

If we can disregard the original human context of the biblical writings, how can anyone ever claim that somebody else's interpretation of the Bible is false? We could perhaps still apply our critical principles in order to see what the authors thought they were saying, or how the texts would probably have been understood in their original context. However, this would ultimately be irrelevant, because such principles would not give us any insight as to what God was trying to communicate when he inspired the writing. If Deuteronomy 25:4 is really about apostles, and not oxen, then we are not likely to discern the correct meaning of any text unless God reveals the meaning to us directly.

Depending on God to reveal the Bible's meaning directly to us creates major problems. First, how would we know that we were not merely deluding ourselves? Second, if God directly reveals the meaning of the Bible to Christian readers, then why do so many sincere Christians come away with conflicting interpretations? Finally, if the meaning of the Bible has nothing to do with what the human authors thought they were writing, how can we possibly confirm or disconfirm even the wildest interpretations of the Bible that we may encounter? Whose standard will we use?

Think back to Augustine's interpretation of Jesus' parable about the Good Samaritan. On what grounds can we say that Augustine's allegorical interpretation is incorrect? We can be quite sure that Jesus was not talking about Adam and Paul when he told this story, but *how* do we know? Perhaps we could appeal to the historical-critical method, but notice that in order for this method to be useful, we need to assume in advance that the meaning of the text depends on how it was intended to be understood by its original audience. Is this assumption even correct?

Naïve Realism

One misguided approach to interpreting literature says that all we have to do to understand a text is to read it and see what the author is telling us. Whatever the author says, that is the text's objective meaning. We could call this view "naïve realism."[5] It is realism because it assumes that the meaning is determined by the text's original context. In other words, the meaning exists "out there" in reality, independently of our minds, and we discover it rather than create it. But this view is also naïve because it assumes that our perceptions give us direct access to what is "out there" in reality, and that our perception of reality cannot be significantly affected by our own preconceptions and expectations.

Naïve realism is reminiscent of the empiricist philosophy described in the first chapter. That view held that all of our knowledge was derived from experience, which implies that we can understand the data provided to us by our senses apart from any pre-existing theories. It assumes that experience gives us direct access to "the facts." A naïve realist approach to interpreting literature likewise assumes that we have direct access to the meaning of a text. To understand the problems with naïve realism, it might help to begin with a brief critique of empiricism.

At first glance, empiricism may seem like a common sense approach to understanding how knowledge works. We look at the facts, we organize them, and we draw conclusions. It's clear, simple, and straightforward. But one of the reasons empiricism ultimately fails is that our construal of "the facts" is inescapably influenced by our preconceptions about the world. Even at a very basic level, it is impossible to avoid this.

For instance, when we place a pencil in a desk drawer and close the drawer, we take it as a fact that the pencil is still there. This belief is not based on a direct observation, since we do not immediately perceive the pencil. It is only because of our pre-existing understanding of the world, which holds that reality is constructed in such a way that the pencil continues to exist even when we don't perceive it, that we can believe such a thing.[6]

If all of our knowledge is derived from sensory data, as empiricists believe, then empiricism implies that our belief about the pencil's continued existence has no basis. We can only accept the pencil's continued existence as a "fact" if we allow our preconceptions about reality to play a role in our understanding of the world. An empiricist who believes that the pencil is still there only does so by smuggling certain assumptions into their assessment of reality that their own philosophy does not permit. In other words, a consistent empiricism does not work.

When it comes to interpreting a text, the same principle applies. We do not grasp the meaning of a text simply by reading it. A number of other factors come into play that allow us to discern the meaning. To think that we have direct access to a text's meaning is naïve because it assumes that our understanding of a text is unaffected by the ideas we already carry with us in our minds. This assumption is misguided because there are many factors that can distort our interpretation of a text. I will name four.

First, our understanding of a text can be affected by our own untested assumptions. Sometimes we come to a text with expectations or beliefs that we are not aware of because they are taken for granted in our social context. These preconceptions can certainly influence our understanding of the "plain meaning" of a text.

For instance, we saw earlier that many people would read the story of Adam and Eve in the book of Genesis and assume, without realizing it, that the serpent who talks to Eve is Satan. In a similar way, many people would read the book of Jonah and assume that it is meant to be understood as a straightforward historical narrative. In both cases, we have already seen how these assumptions could easily be challenged. Genesis never identifies the serpent as Satan, and some ancient interpreters understood that part of the story in a completely different way. Likewise, Jonah is full of details that subvert ancient expectations about the role of a prophet, and is usually understood by scholars today to be a work of satire rather than history. It follows that in order to interpret these books correctly, we have to know if the preconceptions we are bringing with us have any validity.

Second, our understanding of a text can be affected by ambiguity in the text itself. Sometimes a text lends itself to different interpretations, and the correct meaning can only be determined by context clues which are not immediately available to us. The potential for misunderstanding is greater if the ambiguity appears to us as clear language. We encounter this particular problem all the time in our collective experience of sending each other text messages.

Once I was making plans with a friend via text, and we realized that part of our initial plan needed to change, but we weren't sure what to do. I had to put my phone down for a while (the horror), so I told my friend, "We'll figure it out." The only problem is, I accidentally omitted the apostrophe, so it actually said, "Well figure it out." It is a slight difference, but on my friend's end, the message she received completely changed the tone of the conversation. For no apparent reason, I had suddenly lost my patience with her. A few hours later, I realized what had happened and cleared everything up quickly, much to her relief.

Most people have undoubtedly had a similar kind of experience. Maybe it was a text from a friend or an email from a boss, but we all know the panic of trying to figure out the meaning "behind" a message whose wording lends itself to drastically different interpretations. Interpreting a text message from your parents may present the biggest hermeneutical challenge of all, since it usually involves decoding a random string of emojis.

We can call our friend to see if we understood their message, and we can talk to our boss to try to clear things up, but typically we cannot consult the author of a book, especially an ancient author who has been dead for thousands of years. How can we possibly hope to understand an ancient author's intention? Can we look through the text into the author's mind? And what if the text was given its final form by later editors? If we get stuck dealing with ambiguities in the text, it seems that we are on our own.

Third, our understanding of a text can be affected by the fact that texts are static (except for changes that find their way into physical copies of the text), whereas social contexts are dynamic. Texts reflect their original cultural contexts, but cultural contexts can change significantly as they become further removed in time from when the text was written. In particular, the meaning of words can change. This affects how scholars determine the meaning of an ancient text, but it also affects how we understand a translation produced by scholars.

I remember once trying to explain to my grandfather why I did not think the King James Version was the best English translation of the Bible. I commented on how some of the words used in that translation no longer mean what they meant in the seventeenth century. I used the example of 1 Thessalonians 4:15. In the King James Bible, Paul says that when Christians are reunited with Jesus at his second coming, those who are alive will not "prevent" those who have already died. But the English word "prevent" has changed its meaning since the 1600s. What Paul is actually saying is that those who are alive at Jesus' return will not "precede" those who have died. I told my grandfather that we need to use updated translations since the meaning of words can change. His response was classic: "Well I don't think the meaning should change." Maybe it shouldn't, but it does!

Fourth, our understanding of a text can be affected by the writer's own preconceptions. This is especially true when it comes to historical writing, since it purports to tell us about events that actually happened. We rely on the author's testimony to learn about events that took place, and then we may try to understand why those events happened. But anyone who has ever witnessed an event that was later reported on by a journalist knows exactly how complicated this can be.

I was living in Baltimore during the protests following the death of Freddie Gray, who died under mysterious circumstances while being transported in a police van, sparking outrage in the community about police brutality, and leading to city-wide protests. Soon after these protests started, the Baltimore police department claimed that they had received a "credible threat" about gangs teaming up with each other to kill police officers.[7] They used this an excuse to deploy officers in riot gear to confront the protestors, which escalated tensions to a breaking point, leading to physical conflict and property destruction. The police arrested protesters indiscriminately, many of whom were held in jail without having any charges brought against them, while the city suspended their rights to habeas corpus.[8] It eventually came to light that the police department had fabricated the "credible threat" entirely (as many had already suspected), but by that point the damage had already been done.[9] The media rolled with the official narrative, leading to sensational reports of violent protestors destroying their own city.

Meanwhile, local teachers provided unsettling eyewitness testimony on social media about how police officers had forced students to get off their school buses without giving them a way to get home, leaving them stranded in the middle of the city. More eyewitness testimony came from people who witnessed violent acts by the police toward peaceful protesters (and in some cases captured the events clearly on video).[10] These testimonies were conveniently overlooked in the media cycle, but they were not missed by many of the people living in the city and witnessing the unfolding events in real time.

No doubt many of the journalists who contributed to the Freddie Gray/violent protestor narrative thought that they were just reporting the facts, and many of the Americans who turned to them for information probably thought that they were getting a straight-forward account of chaotic events playing out in a different city. They would never have known that the police department had fabricated a threat and used it as an excuse to react harshly against mostly peaceful protesters.

I've identified four factors that can influence our understanding of a text. It should be noted that the first issue—the influence of untested assumptions—is related to the other three. If we do not examine our own preconceptions, then we can easily be misguided by the ambiguities of writing, changing social contexts, and the myth of "straightforward" historical reporting. In these ways, our perception of the "plain meaning" of a text can be severely distorted. This is the danger of naïve realism.

Subjectivism

Because of the problems with naïve realism, some might be tempted to reject realism altogether and adopt a different approach to interpreting texts which denies that there is any connection between a text's meaning and the original intent or context. All that we have is our encounter with the text, and what it means *to us*. I prefer to call this "subjectivism." On this view, any meaning a text has is put there by those of us who read it, whether as individuals or communities. We do not discover the meaning, because it is not located in the text. Rather we create the meaning by engaging with the text.

One can certainly understand how a text can take on a life of its own and become meaningful in a way that has nothing to do with its original context. This is easiest to see with religious literature, where sacred texts are constantly reappropriated and recontextualized, especially in regard to culturally significant events like weddings and funerals. There are lots of people who know hardly anything about the apostle Paul who are nevertheless quite familiar with his "love poem," found in 1 Corinthians 13. That passage is frequently read and appreciated in a context where nobody gives a second thought to why Paul wrote these words for the church in Corinth. Yet who could deny that even this decontextualized poem carries a significant meaning which is apparently determined by the cultural context in which it is read?

Here's another example: Several years ago one of my uncles died, and by this point in my life I had long since left the Christian faith. Many of the people in my family are fundamentalists so, as with many events like this, the funeral took place in a decidedly fundamentalist context. During the ceremony, a different uncle and one of my cousins performed their own acoustic rendition of the twenty-third Psalm. I was very familiar with this song because it was one of the tracks on an album they had recorded together and distributed to family members when I was a child. Most of the songs deal with what you might call fundamentalist themes—creationism, the rapture, the threat of hell, and so on. After I lost my Christian faith, I could not relate very much to their music anymore, but their rendition of the twenty-third Psalm has always resonated deeply with me. I cannot even begin to describe how meaningful it was to hear them play that song at the funeral, or how much it still affects me every time I think about it. I am reminded of it whenever I read that passage in the Bible. It has very little to do with the original meaning of the text, and yet this meaning is very real to me.

In spite of all this, there is a major problem with divorcing a text's meaning from its original context. Imagine a college professor who writes a book about how to interpret literature. As a staunch subjectivist, his central argument is that a text's meaning has nothing to do with what the author intended to communicate. Now suppose one of his students stops by his office to tell him how much she liked his book. He is overwhelmed with delight to hear this news. Then, as she continues to express her enthusiasm, his delight gradually turns to frustration as he realizes that she has completely misunderstood it. She thinks the book's central claim is that the meaning of a text *is* determined by the author's intention. Not only that, but this interpretation has so captivated her mind that it has energized her to pursue a career in studying literature.

Nobody can deny that the student's encounter with this particular text has been significant. It has opened her mind to new possibilities. If she moves forward with her plans to continue studying literature, she will undoubtedly look back at this experience as a defining moment in her life. Is her interpretation of the book valid? My guess is that the professor would think otherwise. But then, so much for his thesis.

Clearly, the realist is onto something. One cannot ignore the author's perspective entirely when trying to understand something they wrote. Even if we cannot identify the author of a text, that does not mean we should just ignore the original context in which it was written. There must be some sense in which the meaning of a text, or at least one of its primary meanings, is determined by how it was meant to be understood by its original audience. Of course, to speak of "how it was meant to be understood" implies a certain intentionality, whether that of the author, editors, or community who produced the text.

At the same time, we cannot ignore the influence of our own preconceptions. Nor should we necessarily dismiss the experience of encountering a text for ourselves and seeing how it speaks to us. The subjectivist approach is important because it reminds us that we are, after all, meaning-seeking creatures. We do not seek meaning purely for its own sake, but because we tend to think that by engaging with other perspectives and ideas, we can come to a better understanding of our own experience in the world. This is why we read books, attend classes, watch documentaries, listen to sermons, and seek the counsel of others.

Critical Realism

While there is something to be said for both realism and subjectivism, to embrace either one uncritically is a serious mistake. There is meaning that can be discovered, but the process of discovering it can be far more complicated than we realize. What we need is an approach that does not invalidate either the text's original context or our own personal context. Such an approach must recognize that people write in the hopes of communicating ideas to other people, and that they read in the hopes of learning better ways of understanding and relating to the world around them.

These considerations point us in the direction of a third approach which has been called "critical realism."[11] When we approach a text as critical realists, we are not just thinking about its original context, but also our own. We try to interrogate our own preconceptions precisely because we know that they play a major role in how we understand what a text is saying. This does not mean that we can attain pure objectivity (as if we could somehow step outside of our own minds and get away from our preconceptions), but it does provide a framework for understanding how we can form actual knowledge about what we are studying.[12]

The fact that we can acquire real knowledge does not mean we simply fall back into naïve realism. I find Adela Yarbro Collins' comments on these issues to be particularly helpful. She says, "We may think of interpretation as a process involving the author, the text, and the interpreter." This process has two stages. As Collins explains:

The first stage or moment of the interpretation of religious texts should focus on the author and the text. A great deal may be known about the actual author; more often virtually nothing is known about who produced the text. The goal of this stage, then, is not only, or even primarily, to determine the author's intention, but to understand and explain the text within its original context. It is in this process that the meaning of the text is discerned. . . . It seems reasonable and ethical to acknowledge the origins of a text as determinative of its meaning, including, as far as possible, the author's intention.[13]

The context of a text—including historical setting, genre, etc.—is crucial for getting at the original meaning. If we interpret an ancient legal code as a poem, or a parable as a historical narrative, or a book of subjectivist philosophy as an elaborate argument for realism, then we are bound to misunderstand what the author was trying to say, and we will never get anywhere near the text's original meaning.

However, we do not need to reject everything about the subjectivist approach. Collins explains the second stage of interpretation:

The second stage or moment of interpretation focuses on the text and the interpreter. The goal in this case is to experience and articulate the significance of the text for the interpreter, including the social context in which the act of interpretation is carried out. It is primarily at this stage that the questions of the truth and the utility of religious texts arises.[14]

Collins adds that it is helpful, in light of these two stages of interpretation, to distinguish between "meaning" (the first stage) and "significance" (the second stage).[15]

When it comes to a text's meaning, some interpretations are better than others, and some are simply incorrect. The only way we can move from an incorrect interpretation toward a correct interpretation is to evaluate the text's original context while consciously taking stock of our own personal context. We want to get as close to understanding the original author's intention as we can, but even if we can't do that, we must try to see what the text may have meant to its original readers. In doing this, we may find that the text has a significance for us that goes beyond its original meaning. In a religious context, that significance may reveal a deep truth to us in a more powerful way, although we should note that words like "reveal" and "truth" are full of ambiguities that would need to be dealt with if we explored this idea further.

One takeaway from all of this is that there is no final stopping point to our investigation of a text's meaning. We make mistakes, we learn, and we grow. We study texts, we interpret them, we allow our interpretations to be challenged, and we form better interpretations. New knowledge is informed by what we already know, and existing knowledge is revised in light of new knowledge. It might seem strange to conceive of interpretation as an ongoing process, but given that we are fallible human beings who "see through a glass, darkly,"[16] how can it be otherwise?

Jesus and the Widow in the Temple: A Case Study

This discussion has involved a lot of abstract issues, so let's consider a more concrete example of what it can look like to move from naïve realism, beyond subjectivism, toward a critical realist interpretation. We will look at a story from the Gospel of Mark. In this story, Jesus is sitting in the Jewish temple, watching people give money to the temple treasury:

> He sat down opposite the treasury, and watched the crowd putting money into the treasury. Many rich people put in large sums. A poor widow came and put in two small copper coins, which are worth a penny. Then he called his disciples and said to them, "Truly I tell you, this poor widow has put in more than all those who are contributing to the treasury. For all of them have contributed out of their abundance; but she out of her poverty has put in everything she had, all she had to live on." (Mark 12:41-44)

When I was growing up, the meaning of this passage seemed clear, because anytime we read the story in church, we would always draw the same lesson. Here is a typical example:

> When Jesus watched the voluntary offerings made in the temple treasury, he was moved by the sacrificial gift of the poor widow. . . . Her giving had a certain reckless abandon to it. She evidenced an undivided devotion that fulfilled the command to love God with all the heart, soul, mind, and strength. In fact, in Mark's Gospel this story follows closely on the heels of the two great commandments [in Mark 12:28-34], as if to be a commentary on them. . . . Here was a widow, helpless and defenseless, who had learned to trust the Father in heaven for her needs day by day. . . . Dare we follow her lead?[17]

These words have been echoed endlessly in countless church sermons, Sunday School lessons, and Christian devotional resources. The message is clear: followers of Jesus should strive to be like the widow, who trusted God so much that she gave all that she had completely to God's cause, instead of spending it on herself.

It seems like a straightforward interpretation, and it even ties back to a passage that appears in close proximity. It also comes with a lesson about how we should trust God with "reckless abandon." As I said, this interpretation is incredibly popular in the Christian world. The only problem is, it is a complete misunderstanding of what the passage actually means.

One clue that we are dealing with a naïve realist reading of the text is the fact that nowhere in the passage does Jesus actually praise the widow's actions. We can see why some would interpret it this way, but it is important to note that this interpretation is based on reading something *into* the text. The text itself does not give any indication that Jesus is happy about what he sees, or that anyone is being held up as an example for his followers to imitate. Observations like these are crucial.

So what is the text actually saying? First, let's consider the full context. Even though it is true that this story appears shortly after Jesus' discussion of the two great commandments, there is much more that needs to be taken into account. The discussion of those commandments is part of a collection of teachings given by Jesus in the temple, where he answers questions and engages his critics (Mark 11:27-12:37). As part of that block of teaching material, Jesus warns his disciples to "beware of the scribes" and adds, "They devour widows' houses and for the sake of appearance say long prayers. They will receive the greater condemnation" (12:38-40). The comment about the widows is not incidental, since it is immediately followed by the story of the widow's offering.

If we go back further in the Gospel of Mark, we find other material concerning the temple. On the day before Jesus teaches in the temple and comments on the widow's offering, he causes a disturbance in the temple by overturning tables and not allowing anyone to carry anything in. Quoting from the prophet Jeremiah, he calls the temple a "den of robbers" (11:15-19). Moving forward in the Gospel, we see that immediately after Jesus comments on the widow's offering, he and his disciples exit the temple, and Jesus predicts the temple's destruction (13:1-2). This is followed by a discourse in which he prophesies about a coming time of great suffering that will take place in Judea, where Jerusalem is located (13:3-37).

The story of the poor widow is embedded firmly within a context in which Jesus warns Jerusalem of its impending judgment from God, and he specifically threatens the temple and criticizes it as a failed institution. Part of that critique involves the temple's exploitation of widows. It is also worth noting that most scholars think that the Gospel of Mark was written either just prior to, or in the immediate aftermath of, the destruction of Jerusalem in 70 CE. When Jerusalem was destroyed by the Romans, the temple was destroyed with it.[18] It is clear that, for the author of Mark (and likely for Jesus, although we don't need to get into that here), the destruction of the temple carries great theological significance. It is perceived through a Christian lens as an act of divine judgment on a corrupt religious system.

In this context, the story of the poor widow's offering to the temple treasury takes on an entirely different meaning. Jesus is not praising her for her "extravagant giving." He is not holding her up as an example that we should all try to follow. Instead, he is lamenting the fact that the temple has eaten up the last of her resources. While rich people can give to the temple with little consequence, the widow has given everything she had, meaning that she has nothing left to live on.[19] Her life is being "devoured" by this larger system that does nothing to help her. She has been failed by the leaders of her community. To suggest that Jesus is holding up this incident with the widow as a good thing is about as contrary to the original meaning as you can get. Such an interpretation can all too easily be used to serve the exact kind of system that Jesus is condemning.

We can easily see how this passage could hold tremendous significance for a modern reader. After all, we currently find ourselves in the midst of two monumental crises. One is a socio-economic crisis, where the prevailing neoliberal capitalist system is draining the financial resources of the poor and funneling money to the rich so that they can grow even richer. (The fact that billionaires in the United States increased their wealth by at least *sixty-two percent* during the COVID pandemic is a damning indictment on our society if there ever was one.[20]) The other is a crisis of an escalating climate breakdown and biodiversity loss which threatens the entire planet.[21] Far from being unrelated, the climate crisis must be seen within the context of the socio-economic crisis, as the global natural environment suffers incredible damage at the hands of large corporations and the wealthy elite who profit off of them.[22] It is hard not to feel the weight of Jesus' lament over the poor widow. It is hard not to share his opposition toward such a corrupt, exploitative system.

In Jesus' time there were other Jewish voices who warned that judgment would fall upon Jerusalem. Josephus tells us of another man, also named Jesus, who spoke against Jerusalem and the temple. This man, Jesus son of Ananias, was brought by the Jewish leaders to the Roman procurator, who had him severely flogged.[23] This adds to the historical plausibility of Mark's account of Jesus' last week, since it indicates that Jesus' critique of the temple played a major role in his arrest and execution (see Mark 11:15-18; 14:58).

Certainly there are parallels to voices in our own society who speak out against the corruption of the prevailing system and who are punished for it. Consider the case of Steven Donzinger.

Donzinger is an activist lawyer who helped win a multibillion dollar lawsuit against the Chevron Corporation for its role in one of the worst oil catastrophes in the world, in the Ecuadorian Amazon. Among other things, Chevron built toxic waste pits with pipes which ran the waste into water sources used by the local indigenous peoples for drinking, bathing, and fishing. After winning the lawsuit, a Chevron-linked judge placed Donzinger under house arrest for over two years on misdemeanor charges, even though the maximum limit for such charges is sixth months.[24] It is a blatant display of corruption. And yet (at the time of this writing) the United States Department of Justice has rejected Donziger's claim that his prosecution by private attorneys violates his constitutional rights.[25] It seems that the administration is bent on serving Chevron's interests.

Many of us feel a combined sense of existential dread about these realities, mixed with hope that those who perpetuate these crises and ruin people's lives for their own material benefit will someday be held accountable, and maybe that those who are currently suffering will find relief. A subjectivist reading of Mark 12 might allow us to have a similar response to the text, but a critical realist reading allows us to see this response as being reflective of the ancient author's context, and probably Jesus' personal context as well. Somehow, through a gap of about two millennia, we have connected in a powerful way with the real experience of an ancient community.

Meaning and Inerrancy

We have taken a long but necessary diversion to talk about texts and meaning, and now we must bring it back around to our main subject. When we ask if a text contains an error or contradiction, it seems clear that, for inerrantists, we are talking about the first stage of interpretation, that is, the meaning stage. Their concern is to deny that the original meaning of a biblical text could ever be wrong. This is not how most ancient Christians approached scripture. By consciously looking past the literal, historical meaning in favor of allegorical or typological meanings, it seems that they would have located the unerring truth of scripture in the second stage of interpretation, the significance stage, although they would not have articulated it that way.

This does not mean that ancient Christians had no use for the literal or intended meaning. Some ancient interpreters were fiercely critical of allegorical interpretations and opted for a style of hermeneutics that looks very much like an early version of historical criticism.[26] But for many other ancient Christians, it did not necessarily matter if the literal, historical meaning of certain biblical texts contained errors or contradictions. These would merely be taken as signs that the real meaning lay beyond the literal meaning.

In order for the doctrine of biblical inerrancy to work, the truth or falsehood of the doctrine must be determined by focusing on the original meaning of a text, rather than its significance. What did the text mean in its original context? What was the author trying to say? How would these words have been understood by their original audience? It may not always be possible to answer these questions with great clarity. Nevertheless, if we do come across any passage in the Bible (even just one) that can be plausibly interpreted as affirming a falsehood, either by making a mistake or by teaching something which is false, then it is reasonable to conclude that the Bible is not inerrant. Additionally, if the authors make any false statements related to ethics or theology, then the Bible is not inerrant or infallible even in the more restricted sense.

Chapter Six

Can Inerrancy Be Falsified?

Probably one of the strangest debates I have ever encountered took place in 2011 between Bart Ehrman, an agnostic, and Craig Evans, an evangelical Christian. The debate concerned the question of whether the Bible can be trusted to provide reliable historical information about Jesus. Both men are widely respected New Testament scholars, and both are compelling speakers and writers on the subject, so the discussion is of great interest to anyone who studies these issues. The debate is available in book form and makes for good reading.[1] But it is indeed a strange debate because, as it unfolds, there is very little that Ehrman and Evans seem to disagree on. In fact, I have never seen another debate where the two opponents agreed on so much. The only thing they seem to disagree on is on whether their points of agreement prove or disprove the proposition in question. Some of the people in the audience probably felt a little confused.

In any debate, it is crucial to have a firm grasp on what it would mean for the central idea to be confirmed or discredited, otherwise we may run into similar confusion. Those who question the doctrine of biblical inerrancy may rush to produce examples of clear Bible errors or contradictions in an effort to refute the doctrine. As we saw earlier, this may prove to be a futile effort, since inerrantists approach the Bible in a variety of ways. This is why we've spent some time talking about how to interpret texts and how to assess if a text is saying something that is false. However, that does not necessarily mean we are ready to start the debate, because many inerrantists deny that there is any conceivable amount of evidence that could possibly falsify their doctrine. Unless we address this claim, all attempts to consider possible counterevidence will be pointless.

Probability and Certainty

The CSBI denies that "alleged errors and discrepancies that have not yet been resolved vitiate the truth claims of the Bible."[2] This is a crucial statement, because it means that no matter what we may find in the Bible, no matter how clear an error or contradiction may seem to be, it can never overturn biblical inerrancy. This is stated as a matter of principle rather than evidence. The doctrine declares itself to be irrefutable, not on the grounds that it can provide an answer to every criticism, but on the grounds that it will never admit defeat. Defenders of inerrancy have won the debate before it even started.

It is clear that the doctrine of inerrancy, as presented in the CSBI, is not based on evidence. I say this because ideas that are based on evidence are matters of probability, not certainty. Evidence can make a theory more probable, and if the evidence is strong enough it can make a theory so probable as to be virtually certain, but that word "virtually" is important. Knowledge based on evidence is always provisional, meaning it is conditioned on the assumption that the evidence has been properly understood and that no new evidence will ever come to light. The implication is that, if new evidence does turn up, we might have to revise our view. A theory that can never be overturned is not provisional, and so it must be based on something other than evidence, something more certain.

An illustration might be useful. We believe that George Washington was the first American president. The evidence for this is as strong as it could be. No one in their right mind would say, "Maybe he wasn't the first president after all. Unless you can prove it with absolute certainty then I refuse to believe it." That would be ridiculous. But we are operating on the assumption that no new evidence will turn up that changes our belief. Granted, an awful lot of evidence would have to have been overlooked or misunderstood in order for our belief to be false. This seems incredibly unlikely, or improbable, so we are right to see Washington's status as the first American president as a solidly established historical fact that can be known with reasonable certainty.

However, what we cannot do, as a matter of principle, is decide in advance that the discovery of challenging new evidence is impossible. Unless we are omniscient, we do not know what the future holds. We may feel quite sure about it, so sure as to consider it a piece of knowledge, and at a practical level this may be all that matters, but at a theoretical level, the possibility of new evidence can never be closed off, because there is nothing intrinsically irrational or self-defeating about the idea. Improbability does not equal impossibility. As a result, even our strong-as-could-be belief about George Washington is provisional. As historian David Hackett Fischer says, "All inferences from empirical evidence are probabilistic."[3]

This is why I say the doctrine of inerrancy as stated in the CSBI is not grounded in evidence. It cannot be, if it claims in advance that it will never be overturned, because this would amount to saying that evidence, which is provisional, has proven a theory which can never be falsified. That is not how evidence works.

It should be noted that not all evangelicals agree with this statement of the doctrine. Some of them see it as quite problematic.[4] Most of what I say in this chapter is only relevant to those who take an approach similar to that of the CSBI, but it is necessary to dig into this one particular version of inerrancy because of its popularity (or perhaps, its wide but uncritical acceptance) in the evangelical world.

When inerrantists decide that no amount of evidence will ever overturn their belief, they reveal that they do not accept their doctrine on the basis of evidence. *This includes the evidence of what we find in the Bible.* That is what makes this such a strange issue. One would think that, from an evangelical perspective, they must have come to believe this doctrine about the Bible by reading the Bible and seeing what it says. But if that were true, they would have to hold open the possibility that they had misunderstood the Bible, otherwise this would amount to the claim that their interpretations of the Bible are infallible. The doctrine of inerrancy seems to be rooted in something other than an assessment of the Bible's content.

For inerrantists who have considered this issue, this is exactly the conclusion they arrive at. William Lane Craig says,

> Inerrantists freely admit that no one reading through the Bible and keeping list of difficulties encountered along the way, whether inconsistencies or mistakes, would come to the conclusion at the end of his reading that the Bible is inerrant. He would likely conclude that the Bible, like almost every other book, has some errors in it.[5]

Craig is not denying inerrancy. Rather, he is arguing that the doctrine of inerrancy is not grounded in reading through the Bible and seeing if everything it says is true. As he admits, anyone who attempted to assess the doctrine this way would probably wind up rejecting it. Instead, Craig claims, the doctrine is grounded in deductive reasoning.

Deductive reasoning is a form of argument where if you accept the premises as true, you have to accept the conclusion as true. Here is a classic example of deductive reasoning:

Premise 1: All men are mortal.

Premise 2: Socrates is a man.

Conclusion: Therefore, Socrates is mortal.

It is impossible for the conclusion to be false if the premises are true. To deny the conclusion, you have to cast doubt on at least one of the premises. This is different from inductive reasoning, where the premises of an argument make the conclusion more probable, but the conclusion could still be false even if the premises are true. Here is an example of inductive reasoning:

Premise 1: Most people who smoke their whole lives develop lung cancer.

Premise 2: Jerry has been smoking his whole life.

Conclusion: Therefore, Jerry will develop lung cancer.

The premises make the conclusion more likely, but even if both premises are true, the conclusion could still be false.[6]

If biblical inerrancy is the result of deductive reasoning, then as long as the premises are true, the Bible must be inerrant. So, what are the premises? Both Craig and the CSBI claim that Jesus taught the inerrancy of scripture, and they believe that his teachings must be true because of his divine nature. The argument would look something like this:

> Premise 1: Whatever Jesus teaches is true.

> Premise 2: Jesus teaches that the Bible is inerrant.

> Conclusion: Therefore, it is true that the Bible is inerrant.

As long as you have good reasons for accepting the premises, you are justified in accepting the conclusion.

But notice, in order to be confident that no amount of evidence will ever overturn the inerrancy of scripture, we need to be confident that no amount of evidence will ever overturn either of the premises that lead to that conclusion. If the premises are based on evidence, then any knowledge which we derive from those premises could only ever be provisional. And if the conclusion is provisional, then it is also falsifiable and the debate can move forward.

We should not rush past this point too quickly. In order to get to the conclusion that inerrancy will never be overturned, inerrantists cannot support their beliefs about Jesus' credibility or his teachings just by reading the Bible or studying the historical evidence. It would not be enough to study the Gospels, confirm their reliability, and then form the conclusion that yes, Jesus really did teach inerrancy. Nor would it be enough to work out an argument based on history and philosophy to the effect that Jesus is God and therefore anything he says must be true. These might (or might not) be good arguments, but because they are based on historical and textual evidence, their conclusions are inescapably provisional.

If this is all inerrantists have to support the doctrine of inerrancy, then the CSBI has no ground for declaring in advance that the doctrine can never be overturned. So now we must ask, is it possible to know that whatever Jesus teaches is true, and that Jesus teaches the Bible's inerrancy, without appealing to evidence?

The Witness of the Holy Spirit

Many evangelicals believe that the Holy Spirit "authenticates" certain truths to us directly, apart from evidence. Since the Holy Spirit is God, and since God always speaks the truth, then whatever the Holy Spirit tells us must be true. This is not the same as just *believing* something as a matter of sheer faith. Rather, this is about *knowing* something which cannot possibly be false. If God speaks directly to us, we do not need to depend on arguments or evidence to know the truth. Under such circumstances we are rational to believe God, and we thereby obtain knowledge that is, in a sense, "self-authenticating."

If God tells us something that necessarily implies the inerrancy of the Bible, then belief in inerrancy would no longer be provisional, and no amount of evidence could ever overturn it. Since God cannot be mistaken, then if the Bible seems to make a mistake, it *must* be the case that our assessment of the evidence is incorrect. It is logically required by the truth of God's testimony. Craig says, "Should a conflict arise between the witness of the Holy Spirit to the fundamental truth of the Christian faith and beliefs based on argument and evidence, then it is the former which must take precedence over the latter, not vice versa."[7]

Craig devotes a whole chapter to the self-authenticating witness of the Holy Spirit in his flagship apologetic work, *Reasonable Faith*. In it, he suggests that the Holy Spirit provides Christians "not only with a subjective assurance of Christianity's truth, but with objective knowledge of that truth." He adds that "arguments and evidence incompatible with that truth are overwhelmed by the experience of the Holy Spirit for him who attends fully to it."[8]

We are not exploring the question of whether Christianity is true, but this idea of a self-authenticating witness to Christian truth requires some attention. What is the "truth of Christianity" that the Holy Spirit allegedly shares with those who listen? What is the content of the Spirit's message? Craig answers, "Now the truth that the Holy Spirit teaches us is not, I'm convinced, the subtleties of Christian doctrine. There are too many Spirit-filled Christians who differ doctrinally for that to be the case." Instead, the Holy Spirit teaches "the basic truths of the Christian faith," or "the great truths of the gospel."[9] Unfortunately, since Craig does not identify these specific truths, we have to do some guesswork. Is the doctrine of inerrancy one of Christianity's basic truths? If not, can it at least be deduced from those basic truths?

Since presumably sincere "Spirit-filled" Christians disagree about the Bible's inerrancy, and since those who accept the doctrine disagree on what it means, then it seems that the Spirit does not teach the truth of biblical inerrancy. But what about Craig's theory that the Spirit only teaches the core truths of Christianity? My best guess is that these core truths would include the divinity of Jesus and perhaps the infallibility of Jesus' teaching. For the sake of argument, let us grant that the Holy Spirit testifies that Jesus' teachings are infallible. We now have irrefutable knowledge of the truth of one of the premises in the deductive argument for biblical inerrancy: "Whatever Jesus teaches is true." All we need now is irrefutable knowledge of the truth of the other premise: "Jesus teaches that the Bible is inerrant."

I am fairly certain that Craig would deny that the Holy Spirit teaches this premise, and I think we must deny it as well. For one thing, "the Bible" as we know it did not yet exist in Jesus' time, since none of the New Testament had been written yet, and Jesus does not make any direct references to it, so the premise does not have much plausibility to begin with. Jesus talks about "scripture," and mentions some books specifically, but he does not say anything about books that were not yet written. To conclude that Jesus' teachings about scripture support a contemporary doctrine of biblical inerrancy, we would have to gather evidence and carefully attempt to draw rational inferences that this evidence supports the application of Jesus' teaching to the entire Christian Bible. Since this process relies on evidence-based reasoning, the conclusion will be provisional.

This is not the only problem. Even though Jesus probably believed that scripture does not contradict itself, that does not mean that Jesus necessarily believed "the doctrine of inerrancy" as modern evangelicals understand it today. More clarification is needed about what "inerrancy" would mean to Jesus, even though he never used the term himself. What would Jesus say about literal versus allegorical interpretations? What would he say about typological interpretations? What would he say about Paul's exegesis of Deuteronomy 25:4? I am not sure how we could answer these questions (or the dozens of other questions that could be raised) without speculating based on extremely thin evidence, meaning we are once again dealing with provisional claims.

Since the Holy Spirit does not teach the truth of both premises of the deductive argument for biblical inerrancy, then the only hope for a non-provisional (and thus unfalsifiable) doctrine of inerrancy is if the Spirit teaches the conclusion directly. On Craig's view, this is not likely, since sincere Christians disagree on this issue. By contrast, the CSBI claims that "the Holy Spirit bears witness to the Scriptures, assuring believers of the truthfulness of God's written word,"[10] and that the Spirit, as "Scripture's divine author," actually "authenticates it to us."[11] If this means that God reveals the truth of biblical inerrancy directly to Christians, then we run into serious problems.

First, inerrantists would have to assume on principle that any Christian who disagrees with the doctrine of inerrancy (or with this specific formulation of that doctrine) is willfully rebelling against God, which seems to claim far more knowledge about human intentions than is warranted even from Christian experience. Second, if God reveals the truth of inerrancy directly to faithful Christians, we have to wonder why it took close to two thousand years for Christians to work out the details of the doctrine.

Finally, we would have to wonder why, even among those who accept the testimony of the Spirit about the Bible, there are drastic differences of opinion about what the Bible teaches. Does the Spirit only reveal a fact *about* the Bible, but not a correct understanding of the Bible's content? If so, then our understanding of what the Bible teaches about inspiration must be based on our interpretation of the text, and since we are fallible humans and our interpretation could be mistaken, our conclusions about how this teaching applies to the Bible as a whole would still be provisional.

Anyone can suggest that God reveals the meaning of specific Bible passages directly to Christian hearts, but then the sheer amount of disagreement among Christians would mean that most Christians are willfully rebelling against God's Spirit, and it is up to the individual Christian to sort out who is obeying the Spirit and who is not. That is a tall order, given that the Spirit is invisible and inaudible, and it seems to move us in the direction of blind faith in the infallibility of our own theological judgments. That way madness lies.

Ultimately the doctrine of inerrancy reveals itself to be grounded in certain Christians' inferences based on what they find in the Bible, and in how they understand their experience of the Christian community. This means that the doctrine is implicitly based on evidential reasoning, and therefore it must be provisional. Consequently, neither deductive reasoning nor an appeal to the testimony of the Holy Spirit can justify the CSBI's claim that no evidence will ever be enough to overturn the doctrine of biblical inerrancy. Perhaps, then, it is possible for inerrancy to be falsified. However, apologists have another argument in their arsenal.

Faulty Manuscripts and Sinful Minds

Evangelical scholars like Norman Geisler treat the absence of the original autographs almost as a trump card for their confidence in the perfection of the scriptures. Since the originals no longer exist, no one can ever prove that an error truly goes back to the original document. Even if the error is impossible to explain away, even if it is attested as strongly in the manuscripts as anything can be, an apologist can always fold their arms and say, "But you can't prove it's really in the Bible." Geisler even makes this one of his rules for dealing with Bible difficulties. Echoing Augustine, he says that "when we run into a so-called 'error' in the Bible, we must assume one of two things—either the manuscript was not copied correctly, or we have not understood it rightly."[12]

This is not the promising route that some Christians think it is. After all, to make such a strong declaration about what "we must assume" about the Bible, we already have to know with certainty, on other grounds, that the Bible cannot contain any mistakes. We have just seen why there are no plausible grounds for such a strong claim. It is fair to ask why we *must* assume that the Bible is inerrant. Unless some compelling answer can be given, the apologist who appeals to the missing original writings is just begging the question.

What makes this even more troubling is that, if we can never conclude that the Bible contains a mistake, no matter how strong the evidence for it is, and if this is purely because we no longer possess the originals and can never prove with absolute certainty that the mistake is genuine, the result is that we cannot claim any knowledge about anything the Bible says at all. No matter what our present copies of the Bible say, we can never know for sure that they accurately reflect the original writings. Far from supporting evangelical theology, this would totally destroy any grounds for claiming that the Bible is inspired or inerrant. Nor could we be sure of anything that Jesus taught, since we could never consult the original writings which tell us about him. If we take this apologetic strategy seriously, we are left in a state of complete agnosticism about the biblical text, and Christianity is in ruins.

Strangely enough, the same apologists who use this line of argument also typically defend the integrity of the biblical text as it exists in our modern copies today. On the same page where Geisler comments that no error can be proven to go back to the originals, since they no longer exist, he says, "So, for all practical purposes, the Bible in our hand, imperfect though the manuscripts are, conveys the complete truth of the original Word of God."[13] But this does not work unless we can rely on textual critics to reconstruct the text with a remarkable degree of accuracy, as the apologists believe.[14]

Evangelical scholar Daniel Wallace appeals to the integrity of the biblical text in response to skeptics who use the same kind of reasoning to make the opposite claim that, since the original writings no longer exist, we cannot know what the Bible really says, and therefore cannot believe in biblical inerrancy.[15] I agree with Wallace's logic but simply observe that the sword cuts both ways. To quote Wallace: "As a matter of intellectual integrity, I would urge those who use the agnostic argument to retire it."[16] Even if the original manuscript of a writing no longer exists, that does not automatically mean we cannot know what it says.

If the lack of the originals offers no escape hatch, then what about human misunderstanding? Both Geisler and Augustine insist that, if an error cannot be explained away as a result of a bad translation or a flawed manuscript, then we must assume that the problem lies with our own lack of understanding. The idea here is that, because of our inherent sinfulness and our human fallibility, we cannot ultimately trust our own judgment about the meaning of a Bible passage—unless our judgment happens to align perfectly with a set of doctrines that have been developed for us by other people (but then how were they able to overcome their own human ignorance?).

The idea that we can never draw a firm conclusion based on our own understanding is ultimately self-defeating. If we render our own judgment untrustworthy as a matter of principle, then we cannot trust our conclusions, including our conclusion that our judgment is untrustworthy. As a result, one cannot just waive away an inconvenient conclusion by calling human wisdom into question. We would still need some kind of evidence or argument to show why a particular instance of human reasoning is mistaken, otherwise we are once again begging the question.

Circular Reasoning

Nothing that I have said so far disproves the doctrine of inerrancy, but it does show that there are major problems with the way the doctrine is presented by many of its proponents. If we can form reliable conclusions about what the Bible says, and if we find an error or contradiction that can be plausibly attributed to the Bible with a high degree of confidence (meaning that there is no reason besides sheer dogma to think otherwise), then we are justified in rejecting inerrancy. Inerrancy *must* be falsifiable, at least in theory, otherwise the doctrine has no foundation.

The problem here is not with the deductive reasoning that some

Christians use to form a belief in inerrancy ("Jesus is God, therefore his teachings are true; Jesus taught inerrancy, therefore his teaching about inerrancy is true"). One could agree with that line of reasoning, believe wholeheartedly in inerrancy, and still treat inerrancy as a falsifiable doctrine. There is a difference between saying that we arrived at a belief through deductive reasoning, and saying that no amount of evidence could ever overturn our belief.

Deductive reasoning is an appropriate way to arrive at true beliefs, but declaring that our beliefs can never be overturned is something else entirely. It only makes sense if we are talking about beliefs that are self-evident (like my belief that I exist) or beliefs that cannot possibly be false (like my belief that two plus two equals four). The doctrine of inerrancy fits neither of these categories. If we begin by ruling out the possibility that any sort of evidence could overturn the doctrine, then we will never be swayed no matter what kind of evidence we are presented with. This is a clear case of circular reasoning. It amounts to saying, "I know that the Bible is inerrant because what it says is true, and I know that what it says is true because it is inerrant, and I know that it is inerrant because what it says is true. . . ."

Remarkably, some evangelical theologians acknowledge the circularity involved in this kind of approach to the Bible, and they embrace it anyway. In his *Systematic Theology*, Wayne Grudem describes his defense of the Bible's status as God's Word as follows: "[W]e believe that Scripture is God's Word because it claims to be that. And we believe its claims because Scripture is God's Word." He adds, "It should be admitted that this is a kind of circular argument."[17] This is an astonishing concession. Circular reasoning is not a valid form of reasoning precisely because, unlike deductive reasoning (and other valid forms of reasoning), it does not give us any grounds to think that a conclusion is true. Instead, we must already accept the conclusion in order to accept the premises.

Grudem embraces circular reasoning about the Bible because he believes that everyone ultimately falls back on circular reasoning. He says that "all arguments for an absolute authority must ultimately appeal to that authority for proof; otherwise the authority would not be an absolute or highest authority." Then he gives some examples of how this might work for other people: "My reason is my ultimate authority because it seems reasonable to me to make it so." "Logical consistency is my ultimate authority because it is logical to make it so."[18] If people can do that with reason and logic without being accused of irrationality, Grudem argues, then people can do it with the Bible.

This response does not make much sense. Having admitted that his whole worldview is ultimately based on circular reasoning, Grudem is no longer in a position to criticize the errors of other people's worldviews. Even worse, having suggested that *all* worldviews are based on circular reasoning, Grudem has implicitly claimed that all worldviews are ultimately irrational. In that case, what point is there in commenting on which ideas should be accepted and which should be rejected?

By claiming that everyone ultimately relies on circular reasoning, Grudem is making an argument that there are no valid arguments. The correct response to this is not to give up on trying to think reasonably. Instead, if a theory defeats itself, then we must try to find a better theory. A theory that all theories are irrational cannot redeem itself through further theorizing. As C. S. Lewis says, "If the value of our reasoning is in doubt, you cannot try to establish it by reasoning."[19]

Perhaps Grudem would reply that the value of reasoning is less important to him because reason is not his ultimate authority. He might say that by appealing to reason, I am making reason my ultimate authority, which is just as circular. But notice that I am not arguing for reason as an ultimate authority. The validity of reasoning (in the sense of drawing valid inferences) is implicitly granted in *all* theories, even those that try to explicitly deny it. Grudem's whole project of laying out a systematic theology which conforms to the Bible's teaching would be impossible if human reason were not already accepted as valid, otherwise no one would be able to determine if two ideas were compatible with each other, much less if certain ideas were compatible with biblical teaching. If we cannot draw valid inferences, then all worldviews are hopeless. Since Grudem thinks his worldview is grounded in truth, then in spite of what he admits about circular reasoning, he has to proceed as if he is allowed to draw valid inferences.

This does not amount to an argument that "we must keep our thoughts reasonable because it is reasonable to do so." That would indeed be circular thinking. Rather, if we abandon reason, we have to abandon every attempt to speak meaningfully about the world, since speaking meaningfully about the world depends on our ability to make valid inferences. Since we cannot abandon our attempts to speak meaningfully about the world (and surely we ought not to do this), we have to build a careful, critical acceptance of reason into our worldview, at least if we want our worldview to be grounded in reality. Reason clearly has a fundamental role to play in our thinking, no matter what level of "authority" we grant it.

We are nowhere near committing ourselves to the sort of philosophy which holds that all beliefs must be "proven" by reason in order to be accepted. There is much that we are right to accept that cannot be established through reason, such as our sensory experience of the world. Only the most hard-nosed philosophers will tell you that accepting our sensory experience as reliable data about the world is unreasonable. Of course, the moment they step away from their computers to go for a walk they will find themselves doing the same thing they just criticized. If, for the sake of consistency, they use this experience to infer that none of us can make valid inferences about the world, their argument will be self-defeating, since it rests on inferences based on their own experience. (Even worse, if they refuse to trust their sensory experience while they are out walking along a busy street, it is likely to be self-defeating in a much more fatal way.) We do not need to limit ourselves to beliefs which can be proven through reason. However, that does not mean it is wise to believe things we know to be unreasonable.

Grudem has done us an enormous favor by highlighting the circularity of using the Bible's teachings to prove the reliability of the Bible's teachings. Since it is circular reasoning, we must reject it, but then we must ask how the doctrine of biblical inerrancy can hope to be justified, if we are to avoid thinking in a circle. The answer is clear: The doctrine of inerrancy claims that the Bible contains no errors, contradictions, or false teachings of any kind. Logically there is nothing incoherent about this idea. Textual criticism provides us with solid ground for drawing firm conclusions about what the Bible says, and the doctrine of inerrancy hinges on accepting this point. This means that we can evaluate the doctrine by checking it against the content of the Bible to see if it holds up. Since the credibility of the doctrine depends on the strength of the evidence, it must be falsifiable.

Furthermore, a Christian can continue to believe that biblical inerrancy is grounded in Jesus' infallibility and his teachings about scripture. As long as they have good reasons to hold these beliefs, and do not have any good reason to think that there are errors or contradictions in the Bible, they are justified in believing in biblical inerrancy.

On the other hand, if we happen to find even a single case in which the Bible contradicts itself or affirms something that is false, and if there is no reason to think that we have misunderstood the text, or that our copy of the Bible is defective, then that would seem like a sufficient refutation of the doctrine. To be clear, we are

ing for absolute certainty. We are just looking to see which
vidence points. If it points away from inerrancy, then the
Christian must figure out what to do with their deductive argument. If the conclusion of that argument is false, then at least one of the premises must be false. Either Jesus' teachings are not always true, or he did not teach biblical inerrancy, or both. But that is up to the Christian to decide.

Chapter Seven

Can Inerrancy Be Justified?

It is a strange thing for anyone to claim that a large collection of ancient writings contains no errors of any kind—no historical inaccuracies, no conflicting perspectives, and no outdated moral or religious perspectives. This is not the sort of thing that a group of people could easily accomplish on purpose even in the modern world, and the odds of pulling it off by accident in the ancient world must have been considerably worse. Through no fault of their own, ancient people held a number of assumptions about reality that even the most uneducated person today would recognize as hopelessly naïve. Stars as cosmic beings, a solid sky holding up "the waters above," child sacrifice to appease the gods—these ideas are not taken seriously anymore, much to the relief of children everywhere. Outdated views aside, ancient writers were just like us in that they held lots of different opinions about all sorts of matters related to religion, sex, politics, justice, ethics, and metaphysics. We must also note that forgery and textual corruption were major problems facing ancient writers.[1]

To all appearances, the notion that one particular anthology of books compiled thousands of years ago somehow presents a message that is completely accurate and perfectly consistent seems patently absurd. This is why, in evangelical theology, divine inspiration is crucial for inerrancy. Thus we have Article XV of the CSBI: "We affirm that the doctrine of inerrancy is grounded in the teaching of the Bible about inspiration." If God was not involved in producing these writings, then it would be foolish to think that the Bible is inerrant.

We saw earlier that certain ancient Jewish and Christian writers spoke about the inspiration of scripture. I quoted two passages directly from the New Testament. These are some of the classic proof-texts for biblical inspiration used by Christian theologians. Here they are again for easy reference:

> All scripture is inspired by God and is useful for teaching, for reproof, for correction, and for training in righteousness, so that everyone who belongs to God may be proficient, equipped for every good work. (2 Timothy 3:16-17)

> First of all you must understand this, that no prophecy of scripture is a matter of one's own interpretation, because no prophecy ever came by human will, but men and women moved by the Holy Spirit spoke from God. (2 Peter 1:20-21)

Both of these passages attest clearly to the early Christian belief that God played a guiding role in the writing of scripture and thereby imbued it with a certain amount of authority.

There are three problems that come up when considering the relationship between inspiration and inerrancy. First, there are no reliable grounds for claiming that every book in the Bible is inspired, and if certain books in the Bible cannot be identified as inspired, then there is no justification for saying that the Bible, as a whole, is inerrant. Second, given the way the earliest Christians spoke about inspiration, there is no justification for assuming that inspiration entails inerrancy. Third, the doctrine of inerrancy, if taken seriously *on its own terms*, makes it impossible to affirm the Bible's inerrancy in a coherent way, precisely because of what the doctrine entails about inspiration. As we explore each of these problems, it will become abundantly clear that the doctrine of inerrancy cannot be justified. However, before we can consider the first problem, we need to discuss how the Bible came together.

The Biblical Canon

The Bible is not just one book; it is a collection of books. When Christians say that "the Bible" is inspired, what they really mean is that every book contained within the Bible is inspired. If the Bible is inspired, then we need to know which books actually belong in the Bible. This raises the question of the biblical canon. The word "canon," in this context, refers to a fixed list—in this case, the list of books which have a rightful place in the Bible. This is why scholars differentiate between canonical Gospels (such as Matthew) and non-canonical Gospels (such as *Thomas*). If every book in the canon is inspired, then in order for the doctrine of inerrancy to be justified, we need to know how a book's canonical status is determined.

Christians do not agree with each other about the precise limits of the biblical canon. The vast majority of Christians accept the same twenty-seven books for the New Testament, though there are some exceptions, particularly in certain Syriac and Ethiopian Christian communities.[2] Notably, the Ethiopian Orthodox Tewahedo Church counts an additional eight books as part of the New Testament.[3] There is much wider disagreement among Christians concerning the Old Testament. The Catholic version of the Old Testament is longer than the Protestant version, and the Greek Orthodox version is longer than both. The variations concern not just different lists of books, but different versions of some of the books they all have in common.

Disagreements concerning the canon are not a modern development. In the early church, there were lots of different views about which books should be regarded as authoritative scripture, and not everyone was comfortable with all of the books that were ultimately included in the New Testament. Eusebius, writing in the fourth century CE, mentions that some of the books which now appear in the New Testament were disputed, including Jude and 2 Peter. He also points out that some Christian communities rejected the book of Revelation.[4] In fact, he says that opinion on Revelation is "evenly divided."[5]

Part of the reason the early Christians desired an official canon is that certain "heretical" Christian leaders were already circulating their own lists of authoritative books.[6] Still, it took time for the New Testament to take shape. The earliest known instance in which a Christian identified the twenty-seven books of the New Testament, *with no additional books named*, is in a letter from Athanasius written in 367 CE. Nevertheless, debate continued after this letter was written.

If we go by traditional Christian views of authorship, the New Testament includes one Gospel from Matthew, one Gospel from Mark, one Gospel and one history of the early church from Luke, one Gospel and three letters from John, thirteen letters from Paul, one letter from James, two letters from Peter, and one letter from Jude. Here we can see the importance of apostolic authority. Matthew, John, and Peter were disciples of Jesus; James and Jude were brothers of Jesus; Paul claimed to have seen Jesus after his resurrection; and all of them were regarded as apostles. Additionally, Christian tradition has held that Mark was Peter's translator or secretary and that Luke was Paul's close friend and traveling companion.

The two remaining books of the New Testament are the letter to the Hebrews and the book of Revelation. Many early Christians regarded Hebrews as a letter from Paul, although this claim is now unanimously rejected (except by some fundamentalist pastors). Meanwhile, the book of Revelation claims to be written by a man named John, and traditionally Christians have been divided as to whether this was John the apostle or a different John.[7]

So how did the New Testament canon come together? There were several "tests" that a writing had to pass in order to be regarded as canonical in the eyes of the early Christian community. These tests were not applied in a mechanical or scientific fashion, and not every canonical book passed every test. Rather, if a book passed any of the tests, then its eventual acceptance into the canon became more likely, although only one test guaranteed inclusion.

The test that guaranteed a book's inclusion in the New Testament was that of "apostolicity," in other words, its authorship by an apostle.[8] Since they were authorized by Jesus to carry on his ministry,[9] their writings possessed tremendous authority over the Christian community. Of course, there were books not written by apostles (such as the Gospel of Luke) that were accepted as part of the New Testament in spite of this fact. Apostolicity was not the only consideration in developing the canon. However, if a book was widely regarded to have been written by an apostle, there was no question as to its canonical status.

The second test for inclusion in the canon was "catholicity," or Christian consensus.[10] If a book was accepted as authoritative by a great number of churches for a long enough period of time, then the book had a much better chance of being accepted as canonical. So, for example, even though there were many Christians who denied (or at least questioned) the apostolicity of the book of Hebrews, it was used widely enough and had been long enough regarded as authoritative that it was ultimately granted canonical status. However, a book by one of the church fathers, such as Tertullian or Irenaeus, while it may have been deemed authoritative in its own way, would not have been accepted as authoritative scripture because it was too far removed from the time when the apostles lived.

The formation of the New Testament corresponds to the development of what we today call "Christian orthodoxy." The word "orthodoxy" means "right belief." The opposite of orthodoxy would be heresy. By the time the New Testament took its shape, a basic set of ideas had become widely regarded in the Christian community as essential doctrines, such as the Trinity and the bodily resurrection of Jesus. Thus, the third test for a book's inclusion in the canon was orthodoxy, that is, the book's conformity to the so-called "rule of faith." In other words, it had to be congruous with the general teachings of the church.[11] If a book promoted an idea that was widely regarded by Christians to be heretical, then it effectively excluded itself from the canon. For example, even though the *Gospel of Thomas* was used by certain "Gnostic" Christians, Gnosticism was widely rejected in the early church, and so *Thomas* never became part of the New Testament.

It was not until the end of the fourth century that the New Testament was formally recognized, thanks in part to the influence of Augustine. Still, this did not resolve the matter for all Christian communities.[12] For example, in more than one hundred surviving manuscripts of the Latin Vulgate (the famous Latin translation produced by Jerome), as well as in manuscripts of other versions, the New Testament is found to contain the *Letter to the Laodiceans*, a book which claims to be written by Paul but is universally recognized today as a forgery.[13]

As for the Old Testament canon, there is no consensus about when the exact boundaries of the Hebrew Bible were fixed, and it may not have happened until after the birth of Christianity.[14] Even so, most of the books were widely accepted as scripture by the time Jesus was born. In order to see this, it is important to recognize that the Hebrew Bible consists of three sections: the Law, the Prophets, and the Writings. The Law and the Prophets are well attested in the New Testament, and although "the Writings" are not referenced as a group in the New Testament, there is evidence that a threefold classification was known to early Christian writers.[15] Furthermore, much of the additional Catholic and Orthodox material for the Old Testament, which is not found in the Hebrew Bible, comes from the old Greek translation of the Jewish scriptures known as the Septuagint. The Septuagint was used not only by Greek-speaking Jews, but also by the Christian writers of the New Testament, including Paul.[16] However, the Protestant Old Testament contains only the material found in the Hebrew Bible.

The Problem of an Incomplete Canon

It is one thing to know how the canon came together; it is quite another thing to know if the canonical books are truly inspired. We know that most of the early Christians regarded most of the biblical writings as inspired, but how can we know if they were right? And how can we be sure about which biblical canon is the correct one?

One strategy for defending the inspiration of the Protestant Old Testament is to appeal to the testimony of the New Testament. Evangelicals often point out that Jesus and the New Testament authors frequently quote the Hebrew Bible as scripture. From this they can generate a fairly substantial (albeit incomplete) canon of Old Testament books. Since Jesus' teachings are authoritative, this allegedly provides firm grounds for establishing at least part of the Bible as inspired. Wayne Grudem makes some bold claims here:

Jesus and the earliest generations of New Testament Christians accepted all the books found in the Hebrew Bible, no more and no less, as their "Old Testament." . . . The absence of any such reference to other literature as divinely authoritative, and the extremely frequent reference to hundreds of places in the Old Testament as divinely authoritative, gives strong confirmation to the fact that the New Testament authors agreed that the established Old Testament canon, no more and no less, was to be taken as God's very words.[17]

These words are incredibly misleading. There are two problems with Grudem's reference to "the established Old Testament canon, no more and no less." One problem is that Jesus and the earliest generation of Christians did not refer to their scriptures as the "Old Testament," and it can be debated whether there was a fixed canon for the Jewish scriptures at that point. Another, more significant problem is that early Christian views about which Jewish writings counted as scripture did not line up perfectly with those of modern day Christians. We can concede that the majority of the books in the Hebrew Bible were indeed accepted by Jesus and many of his Jewish contemporaries. But contrary to what Grudem says, the early Christians sometimes did treat certain books as authoritative which are not found in the Old Testament.

In fact, this even happens within the New Testament. The author of Jude appeals to a prophecy from the book of *1 Enoch*, which most Christians today reject (see Jude 14-15).[18] On Grudem's view this does not matter because the author of Jude does not explicitly identify *1 Enoch* as scripture.[19] Yet one does not expect to see early Christians favorably quoting prophecies from books they do not consider to be authoritative. The author of Jude even modifies the quotation from *1 Enoch* so that it explicitly refers to Jesus ("the Lord"), which is a strong indication that he did view the text as scripture.[20] Equally significant is the fact that *1 Enoch* was accepted as scripture by other early Christian writers (such as Tertullian[21]), increasing the likelihood that the author of Jude accepted it this way as well.[22] On the other hand, certain Old Testament writings never get mentioned in the New Testament, such as Esther, Nehemiah, and Song of Solomon.

This means that even if we choose to define the Old Testament canon based on the testimony of the New Testament, we will not wind up with an Old Testament that aligns with any modern Christian canon. Some books will be missing, and one book will be included that the vast majority of Christians reject today. The fact that the canons do not match up shows that Christians are choosing to accept a specific canon based on factors that are not discussed in the Bible. If they are not discussed in the Bible, then it is not clear how the Old Testament canon could be grounded in the teachings of the New Testament. At least to some extent, it must be grounded in something else.

In any case, appealing to the New Testament to justify the Old Testament canon does not work unless we can trust the authority of the New Testament to begin with. Is there any good reason to do this? This goes beyond the question of whether the New Testament writings are historically reliable. Even if we could largely trust the historical information in the New Testament, that would not necessarily mean that the writings have moral or theological authority. Imagine reading a perfectly accurate eyewitness account of the Battle of Gettysburg that ends with a passionate defense of the institution of human slavery. Why should someone's ability to correctly remember the details of a specific event have any bearing on their political or moral judgment? It seems clear that a person's authority on matters of faith and theology is not necessarily tied to their accuracy as a source of historical information.

This rules out making the case for the New Testament's authority or inspiration based purely on a historical argument for Jesus' resurrection. Even if Jesus was raised from the dead, we would still want to know if the writings which tell us about his resurrection should be regarded as authoritative sources of theological instruction. Why should someone who correctly reports on a significant miraculous event suddenly be treated as a spiritual authority? Even in the New Testament, the mere fact that someone verbally honors Jesus as Lord does not mean that they are guided by the Holy Spirit (see Matthew 7:21-23).

Perhaps it would be easier to discern the inspiration or authority of the New Testament if the Bible told us which Christian books should be treated as scripture. The closest we get is a reference in 2 Peter 3:16 to the letters of Paul (although the author does not identify any specific letters), and a possible quotation from the Gospel of Luke as scripture in 1 Timothy 5:18. Grudem also appeals to John 14:26, where Jesus promises his disciples that the Holy Spirit will teach them everything and remind them of what Jesus has taught them.[23] These passages are somehow supposed to indicate that we can trust that all twenty-seven books of the New Testament are inspired and authoritative.

But why should we assume that 2 Peter and 1 Timothy are correct in treating any other writings as carrying authority? Why assume that the Gospel of John is accurately reporting Jesus' words to his disciples? What about the fact that most scholars see the Gospel of John as a heavily embellished portrayal of Jesus?[24] Or the fact that some in the early church did not accept 2 Peter into their canon? Or the more troubling fact that 2 Peter and 1 Timothy are usually thought by modern scholars to be pseudonymous (meaning they were not written by the people they claim to be written by)?[25] Since these are the books in which Christians find key prooftexts for biblical inspiration, what does it mean if they were not actually written by apostles?

Even if these books are authentic, it is quite a leap to assume that one can vindicate the whole New Testament by appealing to these three verses, none of which names a single book or says anything about how inspired writings are to be recognized. In any event, we have already noted the circularity involved in appealing to biblical teaching in order to show that biblical teaching is an inspired revelation from God.

What can we say about the early Christian tests for inclusion in the canon? We can begin with the first test: apostolicity. This test obviously assumes that the traditional Christian views of authorship are correct, so we have to consider the merits of these traditions. Some of the books in the New Testament identify their authors by name: the letters of Paul, Peter, James, and Jude, and the book of Revelation. Beyond that, things get a bit more complicated.

All four Gospels are technically anonymous, as even conservative evangelical scholars admit.[26] In other words, they do not name their authors—the titles are not part of the original writings—although some of the books do provide some intriguing clues. Whoever wrote the Gospel of Luke is the same person who wrote the book of Acts (as indicated by each book's prologue), and he claims to have been present with Paul at certain points in his ministry (for example, in Acts 27:15). The Gospel of John claims to be based on the written testimony of a "beloved disciple" (John 21:24). But these authors do no tell us who they are. It was the Christians living in the second century who attributed the four Gospels, respectively, to Matthew, Mark, Luke, and John.[27]

Before going further, I need to address a possible objection. On a Christian view, if Jesus is truly the resurrected Son of God, and if the four Gospels found in the New Testament are historically reliable, then Christians do have a pathway to identifying *some* books as inspired. Any books written by the apostles could reasonably be accepted as canonical. On a traditional Christian view of authorship, that is enough to establish most of the New Testament. At the very least, we would have two Gospels, thirteen letters from Paul, seven letters from other apostles, and potentially the book of Revelation.

However, it is important to reiterate here that the doctrine of biblical inerrancy does not work unless we can establish a full canon. To say that "the Bible" is inerrant is to make a claim about every book which is found in the Bible today, whether the Protestant version or some other version (for most evangelicals it is the Protestant canon that matters). It is also important to keep in mind that we are no longer asking the question of why the books were accepted into the New Testament. Rather, we are asking how a modern reader can be sure that all of those books are truly inspired.

We have seen that most of the New Testament can be identified as inspired based on traditional views of authorship. However, according to most scholars, the traditional views of New Testament authorship are wrong on a number of counts.[28] Without getting into the details of why, I simply note that on the standard view, the authors of the four Gospels remain unknown, and many of the letters in the New Testament are regarded as pseudonymous. Seven of Paul's letters are universally accepted as authentic, while the others are debated to varying degrees. The authenticity of the letters of Peter are usually rejected, although there is still some debate regarding 1 Peter. The letters of James and Jude are also debated. The book of Revelation is attributed to John, but not John the apostle.

In order to accept the traditional views of authorship, one has to make a couple of questionable assumptions. For one thing, one has to assume that Christian traditions regarding the authors are, in fact, accurate, in spite of the facts that these traditions come from the second century or later and that in many cases the majority of scholars disagree. Since on a contemporary Christian view the early Christians were not infallible or inspired writers themselves, this means that one also has to assume that early Christian testimony about the authors was generally reliable even if their testimony on other matters was not. These assumptions need to be challenged.

Consider the following problem. A second-century bishop named Papias is often called upon as a witness to support the traditional authorship of some of the Gospels.[29] Yet Papias held some rather odd views that no evangelical scholar would take seriously. In one of his books, Papias claimed that Judas Iscariot's body "swelled up so much that he could no longer pass through a place that a wagon could get through with ease; he could not even get his head through." He also wrote that Judas' eyelids were so swollen that they prevented him from seeing light.[30] Suffice it to say, nobody suggests that Papias is a reliable source concerning the fate of Judas. So why should we suddenly trust his testimony when it comes to other historical issues like the authorship of the Gospels? Even Eusebius, who preserves Papias' testimony about the Gospels, calls him "a man of very limited intelligence."[31] Papias' testimony about the Gospels is not thereby proven false, but we do need some way to know when his words are reliable and when they are not, otherwise there is not much point in using his testimony to support the traditional views of authorship.

There are other complications with Papias. He is the earliest Christian writer that we know of to identify the authors of any Gospels, but he only speaks about Gospels written by Matthew and Mark.[32] His claim that Matthew collected sayings of Jesus in "the Hebrew language" does not fit with what we know about the Gospel of Matthew, which was originally written in Greek.[33] In all likelihood, he is referring to a different book. As for Mark, Papias suggests that he was Peter's interpreter who wrote down everything he remembered Peter saying, though not in chronological order.

While this description is compatible with what we know about "our" Gospel of Mark, the reference is uncertain. Even if he is talking about the same Gospel, we still need an explanation for why we should trust his testimony about who the author was.

We know of other early Christian sources from the late first and early second centuries that quote from the Gospels, but they do not identify the authors, and sometimes they seem to blend quotations from different Gospels together, which seems a bit strange if they thought they were dealing with testimony from specific apostles or their associates.[34] The earliest certain attribution of the traditional titles to the four Gospels comes from Irenaeus in the late second century, about a century after the Gospels were written.[35] This is not exactly compelling evidence.

The evangelical authors of *Reinventing Jesus* tell us that "the patristic writers [such as Papias and Irenaeus] were notorious for getting chronological facts mixed up," but then they bluntly assert that "when it came to authorship, they fared better." They support this claim by suggesting that "the early Christians took seriously the question of authorship" (more seriously, it is implied, than chronological issues) because they attributed the Gospel of Mark to an obscure associate of Peter's rather than to Peter himself.[36] The idea is that, if someone wanted to fabricate a claim about a Gospel's authorship, they probably would have chosen an apostle. What did they have to gain by choosing an obscure person who had no apostolic authority?

This argument conveniently glosses over the fact that the attribution to Mark faces other problems, including Papias' questionable value as a witness.[37] It may be that the Gospel was attributed to Mark rather than Peter in order to avoid having certain issues with the Gospel (such as its lack of chronological order) attributed to an apostle.[38] The traditional view of authorship cannot simply be taken for granted and then used to make a sweeping claim about the integrity of early Christian traditions about authorship. That would be an elegant example of reasoning in a circle.

We need not assume that the standard scholarly views of authorship are infallible. There is nothing wrong with suggesting that scholars are sometimes mistaken, but to merely assume that scholars are wrong whenever their conclusions do not align with the traditional views is obviously question-begging. Sometimes I have heard people reject the views of modern scholarship on the grounds that "truth is not determined by a majority vote." While I agree with that maxim, the sword cuts both ways. If a majority of scholars does not determine the truth, neither does a majority of Christians, much less a majority of second-century (or later) Christians who lived long after the books were actually written. This means that appealing to the wide agreement in the early Christian community, as apologists have a habit of doing,[39] makes no sense if one has already decided to disregard the strong majority views of contemporary biblical scholars. The only way to avoid circular reasoning is to study the evidence and see which way it points, but then one has to contend with the evidence that has persuaded most scholars (regardless of their own personal ideologies) that at least some of the traditional views are wrong.

The second test for canonicity mentioned above concerns the early Christian consensus about which writings were truly authoritative. But in light of the point just mentioned about truth and majority votes, the consensus of second and third-century Christians seems useless as a means of identifying a book's inspiration. Isn't it possible for a large number of people to be wrong? We know what the early Christians believed, but we are trying to determine whether their beliefs were correct. Thus this particular test is not very helpful for our own purposes.

The third test is conformity with the rule of faith, or congruence with Christian orthodoxy. This poses a bit of a problem since, for evangelicals, it is the Bible itself that determines the boundaries of orthodoxy. To argue for the inspiration of the Bible on the grounds that its teachings accord with biblical teachings would not just be circular, but it would also be terribly convoluted. And since, on an evangelical view, the wisdom (or folly) of early Christian writers is measured by their own conformity to biblical teachings, this throws another wrench into any attempt to appeal to early Christian wisdom as evidence for the Bible's inspiration.

One evangelical scholar suggests that the canon of the New Testament can be trusted because most of the books have been recognized by Christians as authoritative since the second century and there has been "no significant controversy" over the canon since it was officially recognized.[40] Apologists also argue that the books were widely received and that the Christian community was guided in this matter by the Holy Spirit.[41] As a result, the books in the canon "belong there because of their intrinsic worth and authenticity as witnesses to Jesus Christ."[42]

It needs to be said that evangelicals would never accept this kind of reasoning as validating the scriptures of a different religion. They would quickly call attention to the recklessness of accepting a community's scriptures as authoritative or inspired just because they had been embraced by most members of that community for thousands of years. Nor would they just accept the claim that a particular community was guided by the Holy Spirit, since this is a subjective conclusion that needs to be assessed in light of the evidence. The question is not what a community believes about its scriptures, but how we can know if their beliefs are correct.

Apologists frequently fall back on the view that these books carry intrinsic authority. The idea is that the authority of these books was so undeniable that they commended themselves as inspired writings to the Christian community, who were thus able to correctly identify them.[43] This is why we are justified in accepting even the anonymous, second-generation book of Hebrews as inspired, authoritative scripture.

It is at this point that the lack of consensus among the early Christians becomes a major problem. If the books commended themselves as authoritative, then why was there so much uncertainty connected to some of them, like Jude, 2 Peter, and even Revelation? One Christian leader named Gaius, in his staunch opposition toward the heresy known as Montanism, rejected Revelation as well as the Gospel of John. He was by no means the only Christian leader to do so.[44] Bear in mind that this stemmed explicitly from his commitment to orthodoxy. Did scriptural writings not always commend themselves to devout Christian leaders? What about their intrinsic authority? What allows us to say that the judgment of certain Christian leaders regarding scripture is valid, but the judgment of others is not?

Since this book is not an argument against Christianity, I have no case to make against the credibility of Jesus' message or resurrection. Regardless of scholarly views, the truth of Jesus' message would entail that at least some of the New Testament writings are likely to be inspired, in the sense that they carry divine authority. But even if Jesus is the Son of God, we cannot just assume that every traditional view of New Testament authorship is correct. Jesus' teachings do not provide any good reason to make that assumption. If our ultimate rationale for accepting the inspiration of books like Jude, 2 Peter, Hebrews, and Revelation is that they possess "intrinsic authority"—a subjective quality that would be denied even by a considerable number of early Christians—then these are very flimsy grounds for believing in the inspiration of every book in the Bible, and we are left without any justification for the doctrine of inerrancy.

The Problem of Inspiration Outside the Canon

You will notice that inspiration was not one of the tests that a book had to pass in order to be received as canonical. There is a reason for this omission. While early Christians regarded all scripture as inspired (thus 2 Timothy 3:16-17), not all inspired writings were regarded as scripture. In fact, inspiration by the Holy Spirit was thought to happen in many non-biblical contexts.

A good case can be made that early Christian writers applied the concept of inspiration to various non-canonical writings.[45] Gregory of Nyssa even claimed that his brother's commentary on the six days of creation was "an exposition given by inspiration of God," which should be admired "no less than the words composed by Moses himself."[46] Early Christian theologians did sometimes specify that certain non-canonical writings were not inspired, but this was always in reference to heretical writings. They did not speak this way about non-canonical writings in general, certainly not those which conformed to the rule of faith.[47] In other words, scripture's unique status and authority did not merely stem from its inspiration. Early Christian usage of non-canonical writings as scripture, such as the author of Jude's use of 1 Enoch, gives us good reasons to make an important distinction between scripture and the canon when talking about these topics.[48] In fact, Athanasius (who, as we have already noted, was the earliest author to name the current New Testament canon) made a distinction between inspired and canonical writings, and on multiple occasions he cited certain books as being inspired even though they were not included in his own list of canonical books.[49]

This accords to some extent with Christian practice even today. When I was growing up in the church, people would often claim that God "spoke through" their pastor, or through other speakers. Sometimes I was told that God had spoken through me! This was never taken to suggest that the speakers were authoritative in the same way the Bible was authoritative, and it certainly was not meant to imply that they were inerrant. But although we never used the language of inspiration in these contexts, we did take seriously the idea that the Holy Spirit offers guidance and wisdom to the Christian community through the spoken or written words of different Christians. The only reason to deny this in specific cases would be if those words failed to conform with correct Christian teachings.

If early Christians could regard non-canonical writings as inspired and thus carrying authority (although not necessarily the same level authority granted to scripture), then they seem to have held a somewhat different understanding of inspiration than contemporary evangelicals do. Evangelicals would never regard a non-canonical writing as inspired (except perhaps in the extremely unlikely event that a previously unknown, authentic apostolic writing was recovered).

The problem here is that the doctrine of inerrancy cannot be grounded in the Bible's teaching about inspiration, unless there is a way to prove that the biblical teaching about inspiration is different from the way it was understood by the early Christian community. I am not sure how this could be done based on the limited comments about inspiration that one finds in the Bible. Even on an evangelical view, there are non-scriptural writings which could be considered "useful for teaching, for reproof, for correction, and for training in righteousness," so 2 Timothy 3:16-17 is not quite enough. Nor is 2 Peter 1:21, since (as I indicated before) contemporary evangelicals often believe that God speaks through ordinary men and women even today. Nor are other biblical passages which indicate that scripture (or certain parts of scripture) cannot be abolished or annulled, such as John 10:35, since these only speak to scripture's authority but not to its inspiration or inerrancy.

As a result, if the doctrine of inerrancy is grounded in the doctrine of inspiration, then inerrantists have a problem. Even if we could reliably identify a specific set of writings as inspired, it would not be enough to get us all the way to inerrancy. Contemporary assessments about which writings are inspired (in the traditional, literal sense) are grounded in ancient testimony. Christians today accept certain writings as inspired because they were accepted that way by Christians in antiquity. But since ancient Christian understandings of inspiration were not limited to scripture, and since non-canonical writings are not inerrant, then there seems to be a discontinuity between the ancient view and the modern view. Inspiration does not necessarily make a writing canonical, and non-canonical writings were never thought to be free from error.

What this means is that if evangelicals want to ground inerrancy in the Bible's inspiration, they have to demonstrate that the Bible is inspired in a way that goes beyond what early Christians meant by calling it inspired. Not only that, but they will then need to explain why the ancient testimony is reliable enough to support a doctrine of inspiration, but unreliable in terms of actually understanding what inspiration means. It is doubtful that this could be done in a coherent, non-circular way.

The Problem of Edited Texts

In addition to the question of which books we ought to accept as inspired, we must also wonder which version of those books counts as inspired. Inerrantists specify that only the original writings were inspired by God, and that copies of the Bible are only inspired inasmuch as they reflect the autographs. To see why this is a problem, we must return to the topic of biblical manuscripts.

To repeat a point from earlier, the fact that the original writings no longer exist does not automatically nullify our knowledge of what the Bible says. One cannot use the absence of the autographs as an argument against the reliability of textual criticism. Textual critics labor intensely to reproduce the original texts, and there is no reason to dogmatically reject their work. However, in some cases it may be more appropriate to speak of an "earliest discernible" or "earliest reproducible" text, rather than an original. I say this because, in certain cases, it is not clear what would even count as the original. Since evangelicals believe that only the original biblical writings are inspired, the fact that some biblical texts do not have an identifiable original poses a serious problem.

We will consider two examples. The first example comes from the Pentateuch. Modern Bible scholars typically agree that the Pentateuch was edited together from a variety of sources written from different, sometimes conflicting perspectives.[50] For obvious reasons, evangelicals tend to reject this view. Although the Bible never makes this claim, it has been a longstanding tradition in both Judaism and Christianity that Moses was the author of the Pentateuch. Many evangelicals continue to embrace this view today.[51] This might seem odd to a modern reader, since Deuteronomy 34:5-6 narrates Moses' death and burial. Defenders of the traditional view could always get around this by suggesting that since Moses was writing by divine inspiration, he was able to accurately record his own death beforehand.[52]

However, there are several comments scattered throughout the Pentateuch which indicate that the writer is living at a time long after Moses' death. For instance, Genesis 12:6 says, "At that time the Canaanites were in the land." This implies that whoever is telling the story is living at a time when the Canaanites are no longer in the land. However, Moses is said to have died while the Canaanites were still in the land. Likewise, when Genesis 36:31 introduces a list of kings in Edom by saying that this was "before any king reigned over the Israelites," it shows that the writer knows of a monarchy that was eventually established in Israel, which happened long after Moses died.

These comments were obviously not written by Moses. Defenders of Moses' authorship of the Pentateuch usually concede this point, but argue that, while Moses was the original author, it is likely that someone living at a later time added certain editorial comments into the text.[53] In that case, such comments were not part of the original text that Moses allegedly wrote. This creates an interesting problem. If only the original text is inspired, then what does that mean for later editorial comments that are now embedded in the text? Since they are not part of the original text, how can they be inspired? For that matter, if Moses did not write all of the words in the Pentateuch, how can we be sure of which parts go back to Moses and which parts were added by editors at a later date?

One can understand why an inerrantist would want to believe that short comments like the one found in Genesis 12:6 are the full extent of editorial updates, but not only is that unprovable, it is also implausible. Why would an editor modify the text just to insert a handful of short statements giving the impression that the material was written later than it actually was? Or rather, why think that an editor would do this without making any other updates? That seems hard to justify.

Some evangelicals are willing to admit that the Pentateuch is not the work of a single author, and do not think it matters whether Moses was involved as an author or not.[54] This is a significant concession to the modern theory of how the Pentateuch was composed. After all, the reason the modern theory displaced the traditional view in the first place is that a better explanation was needed to account for signs of editing in the text. In that case, it is not clear what would even count as the "original" text of the Pentateuch. We have no way to reconstruct earlier editions of the text, whatever they may have looked like. Since we don't know what the original "unedited" version looked like, we have no way to know how it compares to the Pentateuch as we know it today. Any view which suggests that different parts of the Pentateuch were written in different time periods is going to run into this problem.

Another interesting example comes from the Gospel of John. During his last meal with his disciples on the night before his crucifixion, Jesus speaks to them about what lies ahead (see John 14:1-31). At a certain point he says, "Rise, let us be on our way" (14:31). This seems to indicate that Jesus is done speaking, but then without any transition, Jesus resumes his discourse. He continues speaking for some time and finally concludes with a lengthy prayer (17:1-26). Once the prayer concludes, the text says, "After Jesus had spoken these words, he went out with his disciples. . . ." (18:1). It seems that a significant amount of this discourse material did not appear in an earlier version of the Gospel of John, but was added in later.[55]

There are several other places in this Gospel that show signs of later editing. For example, John 20:30-31 sounds like it should be the book's ending, but then we go right into the story of Jesus' appearance to the disciples in Galilee, which is one of several reasons to think that this material was also added at a later stage of the Gospel's development.[56] Most scholars agree that John is an edited text, although debate centers on whether the added material comes from the original author or an editor who was part of the same community.[57] This possibility is even admitted by some conservative evangelical scholars who believe in inerrancy.[58] So which form of the Gospel of John counts as the "original" version? And how could we be sure that it all came from the same author? If the Gospel as we know it today went through a series of editions in which new material was added, then how can inspiration be attributed to the edition that we now possess?

Other examples from the Bible could be added, such as the widely held theory that 2 Corinthians is actually edited together from two or more of Paul's letters.[59] Cases like these help us to understand why it is sometimes misleading to speak about the "original" biblical writings, since in some instances, there may not have been a single original version, at least not one that scholars could ever hope to reproduce with the manuscripts that survive.[60]

So at which stage of the editing process does the writing count as inspired, and at what point do editorial "improvements" to the text become uninspired? In the absence of any direct revelation from God about the matter, we have no way of knowing. This is a problem because it means that we cannot regard the Bible as we know it today as a divinely inspired text.

Notice the difference between what I am saying here and the argument I criticized earlier which said that we cannot believe in biblical inerrancy because we do not have the original writings and thus we do not know what the Bible says. That argument does not work because it implausibly suggests that textual criticism is incapable of reproducing a text in the absence of any originals. This is just demonstrably false.[61] I am making a different point here. I am not saying that we cannot know what a text says if the original writings are gone. What I am saying is, if the original writings are gone, and the version of the text that we are able to reconstruct from manuscripts is an edited version of the text, then it makes no sense to affirm *both* that inspiration only applies to the original writing *and* that the edition reconstructed by textual critics is inspired. It is the doctrine's insistence that inspiration only applies to the originals that creates the problem here. If a doctrine insists that only the originals are inspired, and if some of the books in the Bible are edited documents, then that doctrine provides no grounds for saying that every book in the Bible is inspired.

This does not mean we have to assume that the original edition of, say, the Gospel of John, was significantly different from the version we have, nor do we have to suppose that it was riddled with errors and contradictions. However, since we only have access to an edited version of John, inerrantists are obligated by their own doctrine not to insist on its inspiration, *because it is not the original*. To define the edited version of John that scholars have reconstructed as "the original" to which inspiration rightly applies is both arbitrary and incoherent.

This problem cannot be waved away by pointing out that there are evangelical scholars who believe in inerrancy who have no discomfort with these kinds of issues. The incompatibility between a certain line of evidence and a particular theory is not refuted by observing that some people have no problem embracing both. There are lots of people who believe in creationism due to a literal interpretation of Genesis but who also accept the scientific evidence for "continental drift" (more appropriately, plate tectonics), apparently without realizing how incompatible those two things are.[62] No one is obligated for that reason to ignore the tension between creationism and the movement of continents. Likewise, if some evangelicals acknowledge the presence of edited books in the Bible, yet maintain a belief in the Bible's inerrancy, their belief is irrational. Why? Because the same evangelicals will tell you that inerrancy stems from inspiration, and that inspiration only applies to the original writings. Yet not only do they acknowledge that some of the books in the Bible are edited, but they also hold up the edited books and insist that they are inspired and therefore free of errors, even though their own doctrine gives them no grounds for making such a claim.

Although textual critics can reconstruct a missing text from surviving copies, that does not guarantee that they will always be able to do so. If a book reached its "final" form through a process of editing, and there is no manuscript evidence to guide us, then we have no way to determine (apart from careful speculation) what this editing process *may* have looked like. Whatever theories we come up with will have to be treated as hypothetical and highly provisional, unless or until new evidence comes to light.

Some scholars have a bad habit of treating their hypotheses as proven facts. This frequently happens, for instance, with the hypothesis of Q, a lost document which is thought by most scholars to have been used by the authors of Matthew and Luke.[63] We may be justified in believing that Q existed (though this is still debated[64]), but any theories about what Q looked like or how it was composed are going to be highly speculative, and it seems wise not to build too much on those theories. Any theory about how a book like Genesis or John was composed is going to be highly speculative as well. Some theories about hypothetical texts or hypothetical stages of editing are far more credible than others, but we will not be anywhere near the point of establishing them with reasonable certainty. How then can we claim that books like Genesis and John were inspired in their original forms? What sense would it make to build these claims into the foundation of our entire worldview?

None of this suggests that we cannot talk meaningfully about the Gospel of John, either from a historical, literary, or religious perspective. But it does quite literally make it impossible for us to know exactly what the "original" Gospel of John looked like, much less to know the truth of a doctrine that only applies to the original. To declare, as inerrantists must, *both* that the Gospel of John was only inspired in its original form *and* that the Gospel of John as we know it today is inspired, is completely incoherent, unless it can be proven that the Gospel of John as we know it today reflects the original (minor textual variants notwithstanding). Many evangelicals believe that it does, but not only is this far too speculative, it is also rejected by the majority of scholars due to the strong internal evidence from the text itself. That does not mean the evangelical theory is necessarily wrong, just that it is hypothetical, unprovable, and widely rejected.

Once the force of this argument is granted, we must grapple with the sheer number of edited books that appear in the Bible. We are not just talking about two or three books. The full list of edited books in the Bible would include most of the books in the Old Testament[65] and several books in the New Testament. If so many of the Bible's books are edited documents, then what use do we have for a doctrine which only applies to the original writings?

The only way to avoid this would be to say that the texts received as "canonical" and recognized by the church as inspired were already in their final form. Thus, it would be a mistake to try to reconstruct "original" versions since these might be substantially different from the canonical versions. This might work at a practical level (these are the texts that the church has always known, so these are the texts it will continue to use), but at a theological level it seems a bit contrived, at least on a traditional view of inspiration. Did God not inspire the original authors when they composed their original texts? The other problem here is that applying inspiration only to the received forms of the texts would seem to undermine the need for textual criticism, at least from a Christian perspective.

In this chapter we have focused on the question of whether the doctrine of inerrancy is justified. On what grounds can it be said that the Bible is inerrant? It cannot be grounded in the canon, since there is no non-circular way to affirm that the whole biblical canon is inspired. But even if there was a way to identify all the canonical books as inspired, that alone would not be enough to show that the writings must necessarily be free from error. Neither Jesus nor the New Testament nor the early Christians nor theologians like Augustine offer any support for the claim that merely inspired writings are inerrant. And even if they did, the fact that inerrancy is only supposed to apply to the original writings means that there is no justification for treating the entire Bible as inerrant, since many of its books were already edited prior to their inclusion in the Bible and no longer reflect whatever original form they once had.

In the end, it is not clear what the doctrine of inerrancy is even grounded in. It is not taught in the Bible. It is not logically required by inspiration, and in any case the inspiration of the Bible cannot be justified in a non-circular way. This makes biblical inerrancy a very odd doctrine indeed. Why should anyone take it seriously? Since we have no grounds for asserting that everything the Bible says is true, it is probably a safe bet that the Bible is not inerrant.

PART TWO

Examining the
Evidence

Chapter Eight

Jude and Enoch

Now that we have examined the concept of biblical inerrancy in a fair amount of detail, I would like to explore a handful of cases in the Bible which strike me as clear instances where the author makes a mistake or contradicts a different part of the Bible. Of course, different readers will have different opinions about what seems "clear" or "obvious" to them, but hopefully by this point I have set the stage well enough to put the evidence in a clear light. We will begin with a small error that pops up in one of the shortest books in the Bible.

In Jude 14-15, the author quotes a prophecy and attributes it to Enoch, a mysterious figure from the Old Testament.

> It was also about these that Enoch, in the seventh gen-
> eration from Adam, prophesied, saying, "See, the Lord is
> coming with ten thousands of his holy ones, to execute
> judgment on all, and to convict everyone of all the deeds
> of ungodliness that they have committed in such an un-
> godly way, and of all the harsh things that ungodly sinners
> have spoken against him."

The quoted prophecy does not come from the Bible, at least not the Bible that most Christians recognize. Instead, it is found in *1 Enoch* (also called the *Book of Enoch*), a Jewish apocalypse which is not accepted as scripture by the vast majority of Christians.

An apocalypse is a book where an angel, or some other supernatural agent, reveals things to a human being about issues related to the end times (whether it's the end of the world or just the end of the present age), which will be brought about on earth by events taking place in a supernatural realm.[1] The book of Revelation, from the New Testament, is a prime example of an early Christian apocalypse.

1 Enoch had a considerable influence on the early Christian community.[2] In spite of its name, this book was not actually written by Enoch. It certainly claims to be, but even evangelical scholars agree that this claim is false.[3] It is one of a number of books falsely attributed to Enoch. The prophecy quoted in Jude appears in a section of *1 Enoch* known as the Book of the Watchers. This section includes material that was already known in the mid-second century BCE, although the prophecy is part of a smaller unit which probably dates later than that.[4] If Abraham was born in 2166 BCE as some evangelical resources suggest, the genealogies mentioned in Genesis 5-11 would put Enoch's life somewhere around 3400 BCE, over three millennia before *1 Enoch* was written.[5] The problem here is not the fact that the author of Jude uses a prophecy from a pseudepigraphal (falsely attributed) work, but rather the fact that he attributes the prophecy to Enoch. If the prophecy was not actually composed by Enoch, then it seems like the author of Jude made a mistake.

Apologists have two different strategies for dealing with this problem. One strategy is to cast doubt on whether the author of Jude is really quoting from *1 Enoch*. If you look carefully, he never says that Enoch wrote this statement down.[6] According to the evangelical scholars behind the NET Bible, "It is sometimes suggested that Jude may instead have been quoting from oral tradition which had roots older than the written text."[7] The second strategy is to say that, even though the prophecy does come from *1 Enoch*, which is a pseudepigraphal book, the prophecy itself is genuine. Just because *1 Enoch* is not part of the Bible does not mean that it contains no truth.[8] It should be noted that these two strategies are mutually exclusive since they disagree on whether the passage in Jude actually derives from *1 Enoch*. However, they agree in suggesting that the prophecy is authentic.

An Independent Tradition

When I was a teenager, I assumed that the author of Jude was quoting from an oral tradition, quite frankly because I put a lot of trust in the words of Christian apologists. For a long time after that I never gave it much thought. Years later, I came across a copy of *1 Enoch* in my seminary's library. When I compared the prophecy in *1 Enoch* with the passage from Jude, I was utterly astounded by how similar they were:

> See, the Lord is coming with ten thousands of his holy ones, to execute judgment on all, and to convict everyone of all the deeds of ungodliness that they have committed in such an ungodly way, and of all the harsh things that ungodly sinners have spoken against him. (Jude 1:14-15)

> Behold, he will arrive with ten million of the holy ones in order to execute judgment upon all. He will destroy the wicked ones and censure all flesh on account of everything that they have done, that which the sinners and the wicked ones committed against him. (*1 Enoch* 1.9)

There are certainly a few differences between the two passages, but Jude's quotation is still very close to what is written in *1 Enoch*.

Some of the differences between the two passages are simply matters of translation. The letter of Jude was written in Greek, whereas the text of *1 Enoch* is translated from an Ethiopic version, since the complete text only exists in that language (although some fragments exist which are written in other languages).[9] The Greek word translated as "ten thousands" in Jude 1:14 is *myriasin*, meaning "myriads," whereas the Ethiopic word in *1 Enoch* is *te 'lft* which means "ten thousand times a thousand," or in other words, ten million. This is an understandable difference.

Of course, some of the variations are more noteworthy, but they do not suggest that Jude is quoting a different source. If you read through the New Testament, you will encounter numerous direct quotations of the Old Testament, and if you compare these quotations with the original passages themselves, you will frequently notice important differences. One of the main reasons for this is that the books of the Old Testament were mostly written in Hebrew, whereas the writers of the New Testament often quoted from a Greek translation of the scriptures called the Septuagint. The Septuagint did not always provide the most accurate translation. Thus, we get some interesting differences between the Old and New Testaments, such as the quotation of Psalm 40:6 in the book of Hebrews:

> Sacrifices and offerings you have not desired, but a body you have prepared for me. (Hebrews 10:5)

> Sacrifice and offering you do not desire, but you have given me an open ear. (Psalm 40:6)

Sometimes the New Testament writers take surprising liberties with the text. The author of Mark conflates material from Isaiah and Malachi, but attributes all of it to Isaiah (Mark 1:2-3). In Matthew 2:23, the author quotes a prophecy so imprecisely that scholars are not even sure what passage he has in mind.[10]

When it comes to the more notable differences between Jude and *1 Enoch*, one possibility is that something got lost in translation, since Jude was written in Greek, and *1 Enoch* is thought to have originally been written in Hebrew, Aramaic, or both.[11] Perhaps the author's copy of *1 Enoch* was different from the Ethiopic text that survives today. Another possibility is that the author of Jude omitted one or two lines by mistake. Perhaps he was quoting the book from memory and got the wording slightly wrong. Or maybe he intentionally modified the text to suit his own purposes.[12] In support of this last point we can observe that the author changes "he" to "the Lord" in order to connect the prophecy to Jesus' second coming. These are all plausible scenarios.

On the other hand, it is extremely unlikely that Jude is quoting a "valid" independent oral tradition. For that to be true, the prophecy would have to have been circulating independently, by word of mouth, and the author of Jude would have to have known this oral tradition rather than *1 Enoch*. This would be an impressive coincidence since his knowledge of the oral tradition would just so happen to occur during a time when *1 Enoch* was widely known and quite popular among his contemporaries.

Since Jude's version of Enoch's prophecy is very close to what we find in *1 Enoch*, we would also have to conclude that the version which appears in *1 Enoch* was either based on this same oral tradition, or based on a source that produced the oral tradition. In other words, we cannot think that the author of *1 Enoch* just so happened, by accident, to freely compose a prophecy that was remarkably similar to an oral tradition that was floating around in first century Palestine.

Even if we grant that the author of Jude is quoting from an independent oral tradition, what is the likelihood that Jude's version of the prophecy actually goes back to Enoch himself? Virtually zero. To say otherwise requires us to believe that a book which is known to be falsely attributed to Enoch just so happens to have gotten a hold of one genuine prophecy from him, in spite of his being an obscure figure from the Old Testament that we know almost nothing about, and in spite of there being no evidence to connect the prophecy to him. This one authentic prophecy would have to have been passed around as part of an independent oral tradition for three thousand years before someone finally quoted it in writing and attributed it to Enoch. Keep in mind that Enoch was not regarded as a prophet or oracle until the time period in which *1 Enoch* was written. If a prophecy of his was preserved in Jewish memory for thousands of years, this would be hard to explain.

Inspired Truth in a Non-Inspired Book

What about the alternative argument which acknowledges that Jude is quoting from *1 Enoch* but claims that this one particular passage from *1 Enoch* is still inspired truth? It is important not to lose sight of the problem that we are discussing. I am not aware of anyone who says that since *1 Enoch* is not in the Bible, then nothing it says could possibly be true. But we are not concerned here with the content of the prophecy. Instead, we are concerned with the author's attribution of the prophecy to Enoch. If he is quoting from *1 Enoch*, which was not actually written by Enoch, and if he attributes the prophecy to Enoch, then it seems like we are dealing with a mistake.

One way to try to get around this would be to say that even

though Enoch did not write the book, he did deliver this one particular prophecy. But we have already seen why this does not work. It is highly doubtful that a genuine prophecy was preserved independently for thousands of years without being quoted by anyone until the precise moment in history where Enoch was first regarded as a prophet or visionary, and when all sorts of literature was being falsely attributed to him. Apologists may say that this cannot be ruled out logically, but this is a clear example of a logical possibility that is overwhelmingly disconfirmed by strong evidential considerations. (I will have more to say about clinging to logical possibilities in the next chapter.)

Those who do not want to admit that Jude contains an error may have to bite the bullet and say that, actually, *1 Enoch* really was written by Enoch. This would not fare any better as a hypothesis, since it requires us to believe that a book that closely resembles a Jewish apocalypse was actually written (in spite of all the evidence to the contrary) thousands of years before the genre of apocalypse came into existence.[13] In order for *1 Enoch* to be authentic, most of what we know about ancient literature would have to be deemed unreliable. Yet such a sweeping rejection of scholarship regarding ancient texts would work against the doctrine of inerrancy, since inerrancy requires a fair amount of confidence in the work of biblical scholars in order for us to even know what the Bible says.[14]

There is no good reason to doubt that the author of Jude regarded Enoch as a prophet and quoted a prophecy which is very clearly taken from the book of *1 Enoch*. Yet we know that Enoch did not write this book, and there is no reasonable way to attribute the prophecy to him. Unless we are going to give up on taking these issues seriously, the error in this passage is undeniable.

It is tempting to ask, "So what if the author of one of the smallest books in the Bible made a tiny mistake?" The answer is that it certainly makes an important difference for evangelical theology. If a biblical author can attribute a prophecy to the wrong person, at the very least, we know with reasonable certainty that there are mistakes in the Bible, and the strictest versions of the doctrine of inerrancy must be abandoned.

Chapter Nine

The Field of Blood

In all four canonical Gospels, Jesus is betrayed by one of his own disciples, a man named Judas Iscariot. Here we will focus on how the scene plays out in Matthew 26:14-27:8.

By this point in the Gospel narrative, Jesus has caused a disturbance in the Jewish temple. Judas approaches the chief priests and agrees to betray Jesus to them for thirty pieces of silver. The betrayal seems to involve finding an opportune moment to have Jesus arrested without inciting the crowds in Jerusalem to start a riot.

After celebrating the Passover with his disciples, Jesus takes them out to a private place in Gethsemane where he can pray. Judas arrives with a "a large crowd with swords and clubs" who are said to have come "from the chief priests and the elders of the people." Judas identifies Jesus to the crowd by approaching him and greeting him with a kiss. After a brief skirmish, Jesus is arrested and taken to the high priest, setting the course for his trial and execution. His fate is sealed.

This leads directly into one of our main texts:

When Judas, his betrayer, saw that Jesus was condemned, he repented and brought back the thirty pieces of silver to the chief priests and the elders. He said, "I have sinned by betraying innocent blood." But they said, "What is that to us? See to it yourself." Throwing down the pieces of silver in the temple, he departed; and he went and hanged himself. But the chief priests, taking the pieces of silver, said, "It is not lawful to put them into the treasury, since they are blood money." After conferring together, they used them to buy the potter's field as a place to bury foreigners. For this reason that field has been called the Field of Blood to this day. (Matthew 27:3-8)

The book of Acts gives us a different account of Judas' death. (We know this is referring to Judas because he is named shortly before this passage.)

Now this man acquired a field with the reward of his wickedness; and falling headlong, he burst open in the middle and all his bowels gushed out. This became known to all the residents of Jerusalem, so that the field was called in their language Hakeldama, that is, Field of Blood. (Acts 1:18-19)

There are three potential discrepancies here. The first, which we already discussed, concerns the manner of Judas' death. In Matthew, he hangs himself, and in Acts he falls and his body bursts open. This is not a major problem for inerrantists since it is easy to say that Judas hanged himself from a branch over a cliff and the branch broke, and no one can prove otherwise.

The second apparent discrepancy stems from the fact that in one account, the field is purchased by the chief priests, and in the other account, Judas is said to have acquired the field himself. Apologists typically respond by saying that Judas acquired the field indirectly through the purchase of the chief priests. Make of that what you will.

It is the third discrepancy that I want to examine here. Both accounts tell us about a field known to the community as the "Field of Blood," but they give conflicting explanations for how the field got this name. According to Matthew, it is because the field was purchased using blood money by someone who "betrayed innocent blood." According to Acts, it is because Judas died a gruesome bloody death in the field. These accounts of how the field got its name cannot both be right, so it seems we have a clear contradiction.

One Field, Two Stories

The vast majority of the apologetics resources I consulted do not address this issue. Of those that do, I was able to discern three arguments for preserving the Bible's internal consistency. The first argument (if we can call it that) is simply a denial of the contradiction. The claim is that there is no problem with having two different stories.[1] As one apologist says, "Names can have more than one significance."[2]

The other two arguments are based on different attempts to harmonize the accounts. One approach is to say that the passage in Acts is not actually attributing the field's name to the manner of Judas' death, in spite of how it appears. The argument is that, somehow, the author of Acts really is referring to the "blood money" incident from the Gospel of Matthew.[3]

The other approach acknowledges that the two accounts cannot be reconciled, even on the question of who purchased the field and with what money. The solution to this lies in the fact that the Greek words for "field" in Matthew and Acts are different. The author of Matthew uses the term *agros*, whereas the author of Acts uses *chorion*. The argument is that since *agros* means "field" whereas *chorion* means "place" or "small property," the correct solution is that we are dealing with two different locations—a field of blood purchased by the chief priests and a place of blood acquired by Judas—meaning that there is no contradiction here.[4]

In responding to these arguments, we can begin by stating the obvious. If Matthew attributes the Field of Blood's name to the means by which the field was purchased, whereas Acts attributes the name to the means by which Judas died, then it is pretty clear that we are dealing with two conflicting accounts. It seems that there were at least two different stories floating around about how the field got its name. If some people were telling one story, and other people were telling another story, that does not somehow remove the conflict between the two stories.

It is true that a name can have "multiple significances," but this is not the same as giving different accounts of a name's origin. If I tell you that the house you just moved into is known to neighbors as the "Murder Pit," and you ask me why, and I tell you, "Some say it's because the guy who used to live here hosted a true crime podcast about unsolved murders, and others say it's because someone in the neighborhood has murdered every previous owner of the house," you would no doubt see very clearly that only one of these stories can describe the name's true origin correctly. (You would also probably have urgent follow up questions.) Maybe the scenarios described in both explanations are true, but *as explanations for the name*, they cannot both be correct.

The early Christian community gave us two different stories to explain how the Field of Blood came to be known that way. It makes sense that there would be different stories floating around in the public consciousness about the origin of such a provocative name. Nevertheless, only one of these stories can be correct. This rules out the first argument (which is not really an argument so much as an assertion), and leaves us with two remaining arguments: either we have misunderstood one of the stories, or the stories concern different places which were both known by names that translate as "Field of Blood."

One Field, One Story

Nobody seems to question the meaning of the story told in Matthew, where the field gets its name because it is purchased with "blood money" that was paid to someone who betrayed "innocent blood." But what about the story in Acts? Could it be saying something other than what it appears to be saying? For ease of reference, here is the passage again:

> Now this man acquired a field with the reward of his wickedness; and falling headlong, he burst open in the middle and all his bowels gushed out. This became known to all the residents of Jerusalem, so that the field was called in their language Hakeldama, that is, Field of Blood.

J. P. Holding says that when the author of Acts writes, "This became known," he is not referring to the manner in which Judas died, but rather to the phrase, "Now this man acquired a field."[5] If Holding is right, then we should be able to omit the clause about Judas' bloody death without destroying the inner logic of the passage. But when we do this, the result is very odd:

> Now this man acquired a field with the reward of his wickedness. . . . This became known to all the residents of Jerusalem, so that the field was called in their language Hakeldama, that is, Field of Blood.

Suddenly the mention of blood comes out of nowhere. It could not be more clear that, *in this account*, the field's association with blood is connected to Judas' death. Once that crucial piece of information is included, the passage makes perfect sense. By contrast, Acts says absolutely nothing about the field's being acquired with "blood money" which comes from betraying "innocent blood," as it says in Matthew.

Holding claims that it would make no sense if a field got the name "Field of Blood" due to rumors that someone died a bloody death there because, as he says, "There would not be blood everywhere."[6] This is a strange argument. Even if the logic was sound, all it would prove is that the story of Judas' death as reported in Acts is not likely to be the correct explanation for the field's name. But it would still be true that the author of Acts thinks it is the correct explanation. Holding's mistake is in assuming that if the author makes a claim that seems to make no sense, then it cannot possibly be what the author is saying. He is projecting his own sensibilities onto the author.

Of course, there is nothing implausible about people giving a place an outlandish name, especially a place connected with death—especially a gruesome death. Skull Valley, Arizona got its name because, when the settlers moved there, they found human skulls scattered throughout the valley.[7] It would be silly to deny this story on the grounds that the skulls were not covering the entire val-ley or filling it to the brim. The idea that Acts is not attributing the field's name to the manner of Judas' death is at odds with what the text clearly says.

Two Fields, Two Stories

This leaves us with the argument that we are dealing with two dif-ferent fields of blood. This theory is reminiscent of Peter's six de-nials of Jesus. It is true that the accounts each use a different Greek word for "field," but there is no reason to assume that they neces-sarily refer to different locations. I live in an apartment, and I live in a house, but I do not have two homes (the apartment is part of a duplex). In the same way, one location can be a field, a place, and a property all at the same time.

Another issue here is that, even though both of these accounts were written in Greek, Jewish people in that region primarily spoke Aramaic.[8] The Gospels make this clear even though they are written in Greek. At different points the author of Mark (which is probably the earliest Gospel) preserves Aramaic words in some stories, but then he has to explain the meaning of the words in Greek so his non-Jewish readers can understand them:[9]

> He took her by the hand and said to her, "Talitha cum," which means, "Little girl, get up!" (Mark 5:41)

> Then looking up to heaven, he sighed and said to him, "Ephphatha," that is, "Be opened." (Mark 7:34)

> Then they brought Jesus to the place called Golgotha (which means the place of a skull). (Mark 15:22)

This means that the authors of Matthew and Acts were each giving us their own Greek translation of the field's Aramaic name. In fact, the account in Acts even tells us the Aramaic name. It is a name that is still used today: *Akeldama* (the New Revised Standard Version says "Hakeldama"). It is quite easy to imagine that the authors of Matthew and Luke translated this name using different, but synonymous, Greek words.

Additionally, it is worth commenting on the extreme unlikelihood that two different locations both became known as a "field of blood" due to each one's being associated, in drastically different ways, with the same defining event in the life of one person. This is logically possible, but as we saw in the last chapter, there is a point where clinging to sheer logical possibility in the face of strong counterevidence becomes foolish. Logical possibility is not enough to establish historical probability, or even historical plausibility.

This is an important point so I want to unpack it a little. Logically, it is possible that I was switched at birth with another baby, but it would be silly for me to take this possibility seriously in the absence of any supporting evidence. This is because logical possibilities remain possibilities *regardless of where the evidence points*. Even if my mom showed me pictures from when I was born, had a DNA test performed, and pointed out how similar I look to my dad, I could always fold my arms and say, "Well it's possible that my actual family resembles yours and that the pictures and test results have been manipulated." Technically this scenario is possible, but this would be a ludicrous response. It is enormously more likely that my parents took the right baby home, even if there are other possibilities. Strict logical possibilities do not make good historical explanations.

The apologist's theory of two fields of blood involves an incredible coincidence and hinges entirely on assuming that different terms cannot be used to refer to the same place. Since these assumptions are unjustified, the whole rationale for this argument fails. There is no good reason to think that this theory is correct. It is far more likely that we are dealing with two stories about the same place. The idea that different stories would be told to explain how a place got such a strange name is not implausible or improbable at all. It explains the evidence quite nicely without needlessly suggesting an implausible coincidence.

It is also worth mentioning that a specific location in the Hinnom Valley (near Jerusalem) has traditionally been identified as Akeldama.[10] There is no traditional "second" Field of Blood. That idea was not invented until modern times in order to avoid a theologically inconvenient discrepancy.

We are not trying to establish any conclusion with absolute certainty. We already know from an earlier discussion that historical evidence cannot do that. But if we are asking which way the evidence points, then it clearly points to there being two conflicting accounts in the Bible of how a certain field got its name. It follows that at least one of the accounts must be mistaken. If the inerrantist's only resort is to construct a logically possible but highly implausible scenario to preserve their doctrine, that is not a point in its favor.

Like Jude's error regarding Enoch, this contradiction does not seem to have a significant impact on the main claims of Christianity, and an evangelical with a more flexible view of inerrancy could dismiss this as a "minor" historical error in Matthew, Acts, or both. From a Christian perspective, it does not seem important to know precisely how the Field of Blood got its name. Nothing of great significance hangs on it. Presumably the name had some connection to Judas Iscariot's death. But even if it is a trivial matter, it gives us another reason to reject the strictest versions of inerrancy.

So far we have not seen anything that would necessarily bother proponents of more limited forms of biblical inerrancy or infallibility. Still, it is important to realize that the Bible is not accurate in every historical detail. The obvious next question is, how inaccurate can it be? And why should an inspired text contain historical inaccuracies at all? The remaining issues that we will be exploring have a much more significant impact on evangelical theology. Far from being minor errors related to peripheral details, these are issues that call the Bible's divine authority into question.

Chapter Ten

God's Name

The Bible frequently refers to God as "the Lord." In the Old Testament, there are two Hebrew terms involved here. One is the word *adonai*, which literally means "lord." The other word is *YHWH*, which is the sacred name of Israel's God. It is written here in all consonants because ancient Hebrew writing did not originally have any vowel indicators.[1] Eventually, the Hebrew scriptures came to include vowel indicators, but the name of God was considered too sacred to say out loud. As a result, we are not exactly sure how it was pronounced, though evidence favors the pronunciation "Yahweh."

When reading their scriptures out loud, ancient Israelites would avoid saying the divine name by substituting other names and titles in its place. The most common substitution was *adonay*, which means "my lord."[2] At a certain point long after the rise of Christianity, the consonants of *YHWH* were combined with the vowels of *adonai*, eventually resulting (for reasons we need not get into here) in the name "Jehovah," a word which was never used in ancient Judaism or early Christianity.[3]

Modern Bible translations usually carry on the tradition of using a different title in place of the name "Yahweh," which is why most English Bibles translate the name as "the LORD," with all capital letters. (The New Jerusalem Bible is a notable exception.) In this chapter, for clarity, I will be replacing all biblical occurrences of "the LORD" with "Yahweh."

There are numerous passages in the book of Genesis where God is called Yahweh. God reveals himself by this name to Abraham:

> Then he said to him, "I am Yahweh who brought you from Ur of the Chaldeans, to give you this land to possess." (Genesis 15:7)

Isaac uses this name when blessing his son Jacob:

> "Ah, the smell of my son is like the smell of a field that Yahweh has blessed." (Genesis 27:27)

When Jacob dreams of a ladder on earth reaching to heaven, God reveals himself by this name again:

> And Yahweh stood beside him and said, "I am Yahweh, the God of Abraham your father and the God of Isaac; the land on which you lie I will give to you and your offspring." (Genesis 28:13)

Abraham even names one place "Yahweh will provide" after God spares his son's life and provides a ram to be sacrificed instead (see Gen. 22:14).

Consider, then, God's words to Moses in the book of Exodus:

> God also spoke to Moses and said to him: "I am Yahweh. I appeared to Abraham, Isaac, and Jacob as God Almighty, but by my name 'Yahweh' I did not make myself known to them." (Exodus 6:2-3)

This is quite a significant disagreement, since it concerns the question of whether the patriarchs (Abraham, Isaac, Jacob) knew God by his sacred name, or whether this name was first revealed to Moses. God tells Moses that the patriarchs knew him as "God Almighty" (a translation of *El Shaddai*), but not as Yahweh.

Do You Know What "Know" Means?

The apologists are almost unanimous in casting doubt on our understanding of what it means to "know" God as Yahweh. Either knowing God's name implies knowing about certain aspects of his character, or it implies experiencing or understanding God in a personal way.[4] By this logic, the patriarchs did not know God as a redemptive God, or they had not experienced the full extent of God's "salvific" presence. It is by experiencing God in this way, we are told, that Moses and the Israelites came to "fully" know God as Yahweh. In fact, the evangelical scholars behind the New International Version of the Bible are so confident of this that they intentionally mistranslate Exodus 6:3 to conform with their interpretation:

> God also said to Moses, "I am Yahweh. I appeared to Abraham, to Isaac and to Jacob as God Almighty, but by my name Yahweh I did not make myself fully known to them."

There are a number of problems here. For starters, if "knowing" the name Yahweh refers to knowing about certain aspects of God's character, then it is not clear which aspects of God's character had not yet been revealed to the patriarchs. God does many things in Genesis which reflect his character in a way that is consistent with his character in Exodus. He makes the covenant with Abraham. He promises to make Abraham's descendants into a great and prosperous nation. He powerfully destroys his enemies, as in the story of Sodom and Gomorrah. He even sends plagues on the house of Pharaoh while Abraham and his wife are staying in Egypt (see Genesis 12:10-20).

Of course, in Genesis, God has not yet rescued the Israelites from slavery. Then again, since he tells Abraham about the exodus in advance (Genesis 15:12-14), inerrantists cannot claim that the patriarchs had no knowledge of this event—at least not without abandoning their own doctrine. If the exodus reveals God's "redemptive" or "salvific" character, then this aspect of God's character is already known to the patriarchs.

The only way to get around this would be to say that "knowing God as Yahweh" means "knowing that God has delivered the nation of Israel from slavery in Egypt, *at some point in the past*, in fulfillment of his covenant with Abraham." This would seem incredibly contrived. It is hard to take seriously the idea that knowing God by a certain name implies being located at a certain point in time. The only reason I can think of to embrace such an absurd view is to avoid having to count Abraham as someone in the Bible who knew God as Yahweh.

This brings us to the idea that the "knowledge" of God we are talking about is not factual, but experiential. Again, on this view God's sacred name was not fully understood until his power was experienced in delivering the people of Israel from slavery in Egypt. The patriarchs knew Yahweh's promise, but only Moses and the Israelites witnessed the fulfillment. But this argument creates serious difficulties as well, especially in a Christian framework.

If "knowing that God is Yahweh" is tied specifically to *experiencing* the exodus event, it follows that anyone who does not experience this event personally cannot be said to know God by the name Yahweh. By that logic, it would seem that people like King David and John the Baptist did not really know God as Yahweh, nor have any Christians throughout history, nor did any of the Israelites who were born after the exodus. On the other hand, if we say that the people I just mentioned all knew God as Yahweh because they experienced other acts of redemption or salvation (in the sense of being rescued from danger), then it must be recognized that God is known this way in Genesis as well. In praying to God, Jacob even calls him "the angel who has redeemed me from all harm" (Genesis 48:16).

It would be arbitrary to suggest that the patriarchs did not truly know the meaning of Yahweh's name because, even though they experienced redemption, they did not experience it at such a large scale. The Bible certainly does not say this anywhere. The text of Exodus 6:3 and its surrounding context provide no reason to assume that redemption needs to be this spectacular in order to know that God is Yahweh. Thus, even if we go against the seemingly clear meaning of Exodus 6:3 by saying that it was the experiential meaning of God's name that was unknown, rather than the name itself, we would still be dealing with a glaring contradiction.

One significant weakness found in both of the arguments considered so far is that the name Yahweh does not actually have a salvific or redemptive connotation. The name most likely derives from the Hebrew root *hwh* which means "to be."[5] This makes perfect sense within the context of the narrative in Exodus. When God reveals the sacred name to Moses, he precedes the revelation by uttering a phrase that could mean, "I am who I am," or, "I will be what I will be." He adds, "This is my name forever, and this is my title for all generations" (Exodus 3:14-15). God's *being* in this passage ("I am," "I will be") likely implies God's presence, which in this case means his presence with Moses and the Israelites, a point which is recognized by evangelical commentators.

If knowing God as Yahweh "really" means knowing or experiencing the character of God as revealed by that name, then based on the actual meaning of the name we must infer that this entails knowing that Yahweh is present with his people. In that case, the patriarchs obviously did know God as Yahweh, at least according to Genesis. Linguistically, the name has no direct association with redemptive or salvific acts. Inerrantists only make that connection because it appears in a narrative in which Yahweh does, in fact, save his people.

Certain apologists point out that, elsewhere, the Bible has God revealing himself as Yahweh through redemptive acts, which is quite true, but they draw the wrong conclusion from this, because they take it to mean that knowing God as Yahweh necessarily involves knowing God as a miraculous redeemer and deliverer. This cannot be right (at least not on an evangelical view) because there are other passages in the Bible where God reveals himself as Yahweh, not by redeeming or saving his people, but by punishing them for their sins:

> You shall fall by the sword; I will judge you at the border of Israel. And you shall know that I am Yahweh. (Ezekiel 11:10)

There are many statements like this in Ezekiel. It seems that knowing God as Yahweh can occur in both redemptive and non-redemptive contexts. This means that knowing God as Yahweh cannot be tied specifically to a single redemptive event like the exodus.

Fully Knowing God

The concept of "fully" knowing or experiencing God by a name is problematic on its own terms. What does it mean to say that the Israelites "fully knew," "fully understood," or "fully experienced" God as Yahweh? The assumption here seems to be that the full extent of God's character was revealed in the exodus event. I am not sure that this can be defended from a Christian perspective. Was there nothing more for the Israelites to learn or experience of God?

Within a Christian framework, and really within any theistic framework, the infinite God transcends human comprehension. The Bible attests to this in certain places:

> O the depth of the riches and wisdom and knowledge of God! How unsearchable are his judgments and how inscrutable his ways! "For who has known the mind of the Lord? Or who has been his counselor?" (Romans 11:33-34)

This is particularly important for Christian theology, since the New Testament makes it clear that God only truly became "known" when Jesus revealed him, and not in the time of Moses:

> The law indeed was given through Moses; grace and truth came through Jesus Christ. No one has ever seen God. It is God the only Son, who is close to the Father's heart, who has made him known. (John 1:17-18)

This means that, according to the New Testament, God's plan to honor his covenant with Abraham and redeem his people was not fully understood at the time of the exodus, nor was his character fully known. It was only when Jesus showed up that God was truly (fully?) revealed. Evangelical resources even take this point for granted.[6]

What can it mean in an evangelical context, then, to say that Yahweh's character became "fully known" to Moses and the Israelites, or that Yahweh was fully understood or fully experienced by them, but not by the patriarchs? The only answer I can think of would be to deny that the sacred name Yahweh represents the fullness of God's character, in which case one could (presumably) fully know or experience God *as Yahweh* without fully knowing or experiencing God in his entirety. But this does not work in a Christian framework either. In Jewish and Christian theology, Yahweh is the sacred name of God. Evangelicals like to argue that when the early Christians referred to Jesus as "Lord," using the Greek word *kyrios*, they had the name Yahweh in mind, indicating the early Christians' recognition of Jesus' full equality with God.[7] On this view, Jesus is Yahweh, and in Jesus, all the fullness of God is present and God's character is truly revealed. In other words, Yahweh is only "fully" known through Jesus.

To insist on interpreting the word "known" in Exodus 6:3 as "fully known," while leaving room for learning or experiencing more of God, is incoherent. Even if we accept the questionable translation offered by the New International Version, it is hard to see how this can be reconciled with other parts of the Bible, or indeed with the very heart of Christian theology.

A Name from a Different Time

Another argument that sometimes gets used is that the appearance of the name Yahweh in Genesis is not reflective of its usage at the time.[8] A narrative featuring Abraham might refer to God as Yahweh, but that does not mean that Abraham himself referred to God by that name. The author uses that name in the narrative because that is how the author knows God, but we do not need to conclude that the patriarchs knew the name themselves. According to Norman Geisler and Thomas Howe, "This would be like a biographer of the famous boxer referring to the childhood of Muhammad Ali, even though his name was really Cassius Clay at the time."[9]

This argument falls apart pretty easily since God repeatedly identifies himself in Genesis by that name, and especially since Abraham names a place "Yahweh will provide," which obviously could not have happened unless Abraham knew God by that name. If the author was adding the name to the narrative "retrospectively," then in doing so he substantially distorted the historical account and created a major contradiction in the Pentateuch.

In the end, there is not much to gain by resorting to all these strange interpretive gymnastics in order to avoid the more obvious meaning of the text in Exodus. We are left with a stark contradiction between two biblical narratives. Since the contradiction concerns the accuracy of the narratives, and since it seems to be unavoidable, some evangelicals might say that this is just a historical error that has no bearing on the ultimate redemptive or theological message of the Bible. However, we have just seen that there is quite a bit at stake here theologically. If we know that either Genesis or Exodus is inaccurately portraying God's relationship with the patriarchs, especially in regard to something as significant as the revealing of God's sacred name, then there is no reason to think that both of these books are infallible with regard to matters of theology. At least one of them is getting something wrong about God's action in human history. What else could they be getting wrong?

Chapter Eleven

Revenge on the Amalekites

In the book of Ezekiel, God says, "It is only the person who sins that shall die" (Ezekiel 18:4). These words reflect a fundamental aspect of justice: people should only be held accountable for their own actions. Ezekiel's God appears to be challenging a view of divine punishment that is affirmed elsewhere in the Bible:

> You shall not bow down to them or serve them, for I the LORD your God am a jealous God, visiting the iniquity of the fathers on the children to the third and the fourth generation of those who hate me, but showing steadfast love to thousands of those who love me and keep my commandments. (Exodus 20:5-6, English Standard Version)

In keeping with these words, there are several places in the Bible where children are killed along with their parents as an act of divine punishment. A very clear instance of this happens in the book of 1 Samuel.

To understand the problem, some background is needed. In the book of Exodus, after Moses leads the Israelites out of slavery in

Egypt, they are attacked by a group of Amalekites (Exodus 17:8-13). God helps the Israelites defeat their attackers, and afterward he declares, "I will utterly blot out the remembrance of Amalek from under heaven." Moses replies, "The LORD will have war with Amalek from generation to generation" (Exodus 17:14-16). Hundreds of years later, God sends a message to King Saul through the prophet Samuel:

> I will punish the Amalekites for what they did in opposing the Israelites when they came up out of Egypt. Now go and attack Amalek, and utterly destroy all that they have; do not spare them, but kill both man and woman, child and infant, ox and sheep, camel and donkey. (1 Samuel 15:1-3)

There are two problems here. The first is a logical problem. There seems to be a glaring contradiction between this passage and those passages in Ezekiel which explicitly deny that God punishes children for the sins of their parents. The second problem, which is a moral problem, is obvious. God is commanding the Israelites to commit what appears to be genocide. He even specifies that the Israelite soldiers should kill all the children and infants. The logical problem and the moral problem created by this passage are two distinct problems facing biblical inerrancy, so it is crucial to recognize when apologists fail to make this distinction.

Relevant to this discussion is the similar genocidal action which God commands the Israelites to commit against the Canaanites and other people living in the Promised Land:

But as for the towns of these peoples that the LORD your God is giving you as an inheritance, you must not let anything that breathes remain alive. You shall annihilate them—the Hittites and the Amorites, the Canaanites and the Perizzites, the Hivites and the Jebusites—just as the LORD your God has commanded, so that they may not teach you to do all the abhorrent things that they do for their gods, and you thus sin against the LORD your God. (Deuteronomy 20:16-18)

Israel is instructed by God to let certain people remain alive in the towns outside these areas, but for these specific territories, God explicitly commands them not to let anyone survive.

Defending God at All Costs

Regarding the logical contradiction between the words of Ezekiel and the other passages, the apologists have a few different arguments. One is to say that when God talks about "visiting the iniquity of the fathers on the children to the third and fourth generation," this is not talking about holding children personally accountable for their parents' or ancestors' sins. Rather, the children suffer the consequences of their parents' bad choices without incurring their guilt, as when the children of alcoholics suffer as a result of their parents' addiction. The children certainly do suffer, but the blame falls squarely on the parents.[1]

An alternative argument suggests that the only reason that we modern readers are uncomfortable with the thought of "corporate punishment" is because we are steeped in modern Western individualism, something which would have been totally foreign to the ancient Near Eastern world, which was more collectivist. For them, it was perfectly acceptable that children be punished along with their parents for things their parents had done.[2]

Another talking point is that if God visits the iniquity of the fathers on their children, then this must mean that the children have sinned too.[3] If one person's sins bring disaster upon another person, neither is being treated unjustly by God because both of them are sinners anyway. The disaster caused by one person's sin is a fitting punishment for the sins of the other person.[4] Thus, when children die with their parents as a result of a situation brought about by their parents' sinfulness, the children are receiving a just fate because they, too, are sinners.

Regarding the moral problem with God commanding the Israelites to wipe out the Amalekites along with their children and infants, I can discern at least *eight* arguments that have been used by the apologists. First, the apologists argue that Israel's military actions against the Canaanites and Amalekites do not technically count as genocide. A number of reasons are given: Israel was not attacking a group of people within its own borders; the Amalekites were not being deported to other environments or hunted down and exterminated; the Israelites were not targeting noncombatants; they were not deliberately killing people based on their ethnicity; it was about taking the land, not killing the people; and so on. As a result, we are told, it is historically inaccurate and misleading to label the events of 1 Samuel 15 as genocide.[5] Taking this argument a bit further, some apologists explain that this event cannot be genocidal precisely because God commanded it. In the absence of a divine command, perhaps it would have been genocide, but because of the divine command, it is not.[6]

Second, the apologists argue that only a surface-level reading allows us to assume that God wiped out all the children and other noncombatant civilians of Amalek. It is very possible that the Israelites did not actually massacre the women and children. After all, we have no record that they actually went through with such actions. For all we know, the innocent civilians may have fled the land before Israel got there.[7]

Third, the apologists claim that it was right for God to massacre the Amalekites, just as he was right to exterminate the Canaanites, because they deserved it. They were no angels. In fact, they were "utterly depraved,"[8] "debauched and cruel,"[9] "a horde of bloodthirsty guerillas. . . utterly lost to the nobler feelings of mankind."[10] As Paul Copan says, "Sometimes God simply gives up on nations, cities, or individuals when they've gone past a point of no return."[11]

Fourth, the apologists argue that if God had allowed any of the Amalekites or Canaanites to live, they would have destroyed Israel or led Israel astray from its covenant with God by corrupting them with their pagan practices. That is why their population had to be exterminated.[12] If God had spared even the children, there is no question that they would have ruined everything. William Lane Craig says, "God knew that if these Canaanite children were allowed to live, they would spell the undoing of Israel."[13]

Fifth, the apologists declare that God can kill whomever he wants, whenever and however he wants, since God has sovereignty over everything. All life belongs to God, so it is his to do with as he pleases. In fact, God takes every person's life at some point, at the moment of each person's death. Since God is not unjust to kill people through, say, natural disasters, then he is not unjust to kill people along with their children and infants through brutal annihilation at the hands of an opposing army.[14]

Sixth, the apologists suggest that even though killing children may seem wrong to us, we cannot trust our own moral reflexes on this issue. We are told that there are possible cases where it is morally permissible to kill a child, such as unsuccessful childbirths when a man has to choose between the life of his child or the life of his wife. For all we know, there may be other cases where killing children is permitted, and this could very well include Israel's military campaigns against the Canaanites and Amalekites.[15] Furthermore, God's wisdom is greater than ours. If God commands something that looks to us like genocide, we must assume that our perception is mistaken and that the command is justified.[16]

Seventh, the apologists observe that, on a Christian view, all of us deserve to die because of our sinful nature.[17] What should shock us most about the massacre of the Amalekites and the Canaanites is not the fact that it happened, but rather the fact that we do not all suffer the same fate. In light of this, we should assume that God's actions as described in the Bible are morally perfect and for our benefit. Jerry Walls and David Baggett write, "Is it not consistent with a perfectly good God that he would want what is in the ultimate best interest of every person, even if that were to include, if necessary, some warfare along the way?"[18]

Finally, in what is perhaps the most unnerving of all these arguments (though the competition is steep), many apologists argue that the killing of the Amalekite children was an act of mercy, since the Israelites did not have the means to save them. They lacked the social infrastructure to take care of the children after killing their parents, so their only alternatives would have been to leave them stranded in the desert, or to kill them on the spot. In this framework, we are told, brutally killing the children and infants was the most merciful, least dehumanizing option.[19] In fact, since the children killed by Israelite soldiers would have died before the so-called "age of accountability," they were too young to be held accountable by God for their sins. This means that the brutal killing of the Amalekite children was ultimately a good thing for them, since they immediately went to heaven when they died.[20]

Punishing Children for the Sins of the Parents

The major discrepancy we are dealing with is between Ezekiel's claim that God never punishes children for the sins of their ancestors, and the stories found elsewhere, especially in 1 Samuel 15, in which God seems to do exactly this. The apologists argue that children are never considered guilty for the sins of their parents, but that they are simply suffering the natural consequences of their parents' bad decisions. In order to see why this argument does not work, it is important to keep our focus specifically on this case involving the Amalekites.

The apologists often treat Ezekiel's references to "children" and "fathers" as actual children and their literal parents. Thus, we get lots of illustrations about how children today might suffer because their parents are alcoholics or drug addicts. But note that Ezekiel's point is not limited to literal children. If you read through Ezekiel 18, he talks about sons who deviate from the path of their fathers, and then grandsons who come back to the path of their grandfathers. It is clear that he is talking about the things they do as adults. Children are not usually in a position to "oppress the poor and needy" or "defile their neighbor's wife" (see Ezekiel 18:11-12). It should also be noted that the Hebrew word for "father" can also mean "ancestor."

In the story of the Amalekites, God explicitly identifies the rationale for this military campaign as punishment for something their ancestors did to the Israelites centuries earlier. God says, "I will punish the Amalekites"—here referring to those Amalekites who were currently alive—"for what they did in opposing the Israelites when they came up out of Egypt"—referring to something that their ancestors had done centuries earlier. No other reason is given, and that is just the problem. God explicitly declares that he is punishing people for the sins of their ancestors—in other words, punishing children for the sins of their fathers.

If the Amalekites are brutally executed, is that not an appropriate response for God to have toward human sin? We cannot lose sight of what this passage actually says. God is not punishing the Amalekites for their own actions, and thus their own present wickedness seems to be irrelevant. He is punishing them for the actions of their ancestors. Apologists frequently insist that any Amalekites who died were necessarily guilty, and that, had there been any Amalekites who were willing to repent, God would have spared them. But the problem we are discussing here is not with how many Amalekites actually survived (if such a military campaign ever took place), but rather with the command that God is depicted as giving to the Israelites. That is where the conflict lies, and so this idea that all people are sinful and deserve to die is irrelevant to the logical problem that we are discussing. (It is not irrelevant to the moral problem, which is why we will come back to that issue later.)

What about this idea of "corporate punishment"? Am I being too much of a Western individualist? Once again—we are not discussing a moral problem here, but a logical one. There is a clear tension between what Ezekiel says about individual accountability and what God commands in 1 Samuel 15. If anyone is being an individualist here, it is Ezekiel. If God punishes the people of Amalek as a corporate body for something their nation did hundreds of years earlier, then he is punishing a group of people for something that not a single one of them had anything to do with.

In writing this response, I thought of a potential modern day analogy that an apologist might use to bolster their argument (though I have never seen anyone try this). There are many people today who think that the United States government owes the African-American community reparations for the country's long, dark history of slavery, and the lasting legacy of white supremacy that it established. I have often heard people claim in response that the present day government should not be held accountable for slavery in the past, since white people today do not own slaves. Personally, I am sympathetic toward the movement for reparations, and I think there is a lot more to consider there than whether or not white people today have ever owned slaves. Haven't I just destroyed my whole argument? If I think that a nation *is* accountable for events that happened before any of its present citizens were born, yet I also agree with Ezekiel that nobody should be held accountable for another person's actions, am I not caught in the same contradiction?

These two situations are not the same. One concerns a government granting a certain amount of economic relief to a community that continues to struggle under the lasting impact of the racist economic system upon which this nation was built. The purpose would be to achieve racial and economic justice. The present leadership of the country can be held accountable because its failure to deal with that ongoing injustice is what allows the past to continue to impact the present in tangible, devastating ways. By doing nothing, the nation's leaders are shirking their responsibility to the people.

However, the other scenario concerns wiping out an entire people because of a wicked military campaign its leaders conducted centuries earlier. That is not about justice; it is about vengeance. Even worse, it is vengeance taken out on certain people based on their national identity. In order for the analogy to work, the movement for reparations would have to be demanding that all white people living on American soil, including children and infants, be brutally exterminated as a form of punishment for things that our colonial forefathers did. Thankfully, that is not the case.

Apologists might counter by referring to other parts of the Bible where the Amalekites continue to oppose Israel, suggesting that this was also an ongoing issue for which the Amalekite leaders were accountable. The problem is that the passage in 1 Samuel 15 does not use this as a rationale for Israel's mission to destroy them. The only reason it gives is that the Amalekites must be punished for something their ancestors did. It is not about providing relief to an oppressed community. The contradiction remains.

A Genocide by Any Other Name

We have seen that some apologists blatantly deny that the massacre of the Amalekites is genocide. (They typically refer to these events as "conquests" and "killings.") Looking back through the arguments, we can discern two different strategies for denying that the campaign against the Amalekites is genocidal. One strategy denies that it counts as genocidal on the grounds that "real" genocides look very different from this. The other strategy is based on an ethical theory called "divine command theory." This theory suggests that genocide, like murder, is determined by context, and that any context in which God commands an act necessarily implies that the act is morally right. Murder is wrong because you are not supposed to willfully kill another person unlawfully, but if God commands you to kill a person in a way that would count as murder in any other context, the fact that God has commanded you to do it means that it is not murder. After all, God is the highest moral authority. Likewise, what would be genocide in any other context is not genocide if God tells you to do it.

This all requires a considerable amount of correction. To begin with, the term "genocide" is a relatively recent one. It was coined by Raphael Lemkin during World War II. He used the word to identify a kind of crime against humanity that had been attested all throughout history, but for which there was no clear legal definition or accountability. Given everything that was happening in Europe at the time, Lemkin's project was of immense practical importance. Adam Jones observes, "Barely a year after Lemkin coined the term, it was included in the Nuremberg indictments of Nazi war criminals." Although it did not figure in the subsequent judgments, in 1948 the UN Convention on the Prevention and Punishment of the Crime of Genocide "entrenched genocide in international and domestic law."[21]

When Glenn Miller of Christian Thinktank declares with confidence that the killing of the Amalekites down to the last child "doesn't even come close to what we consider 'genocide' today,"[22] he is being grossly misleading. One thing that Miller and the other apologists never seem to mention, which is absolutely crucial, is that genocide is a contested concept. A contested concept is one that has no unanimously agreed upon definition. Other contested concepts would include words like "religion," "miracle," "history," "nature," and "truth." Obviously, contested concepts can be incredibly important in shaping our understanding of the world. The fact that they are contested does not mean that they are expendable or that they carry no weight. It means that scholars who become experts on these topics debate each other on the precise details of the concepts involved. In short, there is no single definition of genocide.

In Lemkin's view, genocide is "the intentional destruction of national groups on the basis of their collective identity."[23] In the time since Lemkin coined the term, genocide scholars have debated different issues such as "whether mass killing is definitional to genocide" and whether it is limited to ethnic and national groups, but not political groups or other kinds of groups.[24] Jones provides a list of no less than twenty-five different scholarly definitions of genocide.[25] Some of these definitions are very basic, including this one: "Genocide is any act that puts the very existence of a group in jeopardy."[26] That definition is attributed to Helen Fein, who, I note, is one of Miller's sources. Obviously this particular definition is compatible with the massacre of the Amalekites, and many others in the list are as well.

Reading through the various definitions, you can get a sense of the different issues that come into play. For example, is genocide something that must be sanctioned by a government against its own people? Consider this definition attributed to Barbara Huff and Ted Gurr:

> By our definition, genocides and politicides are the promotion and execution of policies by a state or its agents which results in the deaths of a substantial portion of a group. . . . In genocides the victimized groups are defined primarily in terms of their communal characteristics, i.e., ethnicity, religion, or nationality. In politicides the victim groups are defined primarily in terms of their hierarchical position or political opposition to the regime and dominant groups.[27]

It does not seem to be a necessary part of the definition of genocide (especially when contrasted with politicide) that it concerns the actions of a government against its own people. For example, the indigenous peoples of North America who were wiped out by European colonizers were not subjects of European governments, except of course for when they were forced to comply with European demands. Yet the devastation of indigenous communities in America was a very clear case of genocide.[28]

1 Samuel 15 depicts a situation where an invading army sets out to annihilate an entire nation of people, down to the last child. It is the fact that these people are identified as "Amalekites"—in other words, their national identity—that makes them targets for Israel's military campaign. Remarks from the apologists about how this was not about destroying people so much as taking the land, or about how the Israelites would have let immigrants live, are incongruent with what the passage in 1 Samuel 15 actually says. The action God is

calling his people to commit clearly falls into the spectrum of events which fit the general profile of genocide, even if the finer details of the concept are debated.

Likewise, when Miller says, "Academic definitions of genocide exclude combat deaths and noncombatants that die as a by-product of military action,"[29] he fails to realize that in 1 Samuel 15 the Israelites are specifically instructed to wipe out all the people, whether combatants or not. By Miller's own account, God is commanding something that looks an awful lot like genocide. Having said that, scholars debate the role of human intention in identifying genocide since certain genocidal events can play out in complicated, unplanned ways.[30] This means that it may not matter whether a military campaign intentionally sets out to target noncombatants. Additionally, it is worth noting that in both Jones' *Genocide: A Comprehensive Introduction* and Norman Naimark's *Genocide: A World History*, the story of the Amalekites is held up as a prime example of genocide in the ancient world.[31]

We saw earlier that on a certain version of "divine command theory," it is the command of God that makes the killing of the entire Amalekite population something that is both good and morally obligatory. Something which would have been genocide in any other context is, by virtue of God's command, no longer genocidal. The action is exactly the same, but the moral meaning is not, because God has authorized it, and he is perfectly good and sovereign over life. God could have used an earthquake to wipe out the Amalekites; instead, he chose to use the Israelites. Does this version of divine command theory hold up to scrutiny?

What the divine command theorist is doing here is trying to show that God's commanding such a thing without it being truly genocidal is at least *logically possible*. But the fact that some form of divine command theory may be logically possible does not automatically mean that the theory is correct. Evangelicals who take this route to defending would-be genocidal acts in the Bible are cling-ing to a sheer logical possibility, not necessarily to a view which is supported by evidence. The logical coherence of a moral theory does not mean it is morally acceptable.

So how do we determine if a theory is morally acceptable? Quite simply, by taking moral considerations into account. This is why we do not need a logical proof that this version of divine command the-ory is false. Reason is not our only avenue to truth. We also have (among other things) our moral experience. It is by moral experi-ence that we can discern moral truths. Since Craig is the apologist defending divine command theory in this case, it seems prudent to quote a point he makes in the context of a different debate. He says, "I take it that in moral experience we do apprehend a realm of ob-jective moral values and duties, just as in sensory experience we ap-prehend a realm of objectively existing physical objects."[32] On this point, I agree with Craig wholeheartedly.

For the sake of clarity, let me quote Craig further: "When we speak of moral values, we're talking about whether something is good or bad; when we talk about moral duties we are concerned with whether something is right or wrong."[33] Moral duties, things that are "right," refer to things that we are obligated to do. We are not necessarily obligated to do everything that counts as "good." It might be good for me to give all my money to a struggling friend, or it might be good for me to give all my money to a local nonprofit, but that does not mean I am obligated to do either, and I cannot be obligated to do both. On the other hand, not only is it good for par-ents to take care of their children, but it is also their moral duty—in other words, it is the right thing to do. All things being equal, it would be wrong for them *not* to do it.

To speak of "objective" moral values and duties is to refer to things that are good or evil, right or wrong, independently of what people think of them. Objective values and duties are not matters of opinion or social convention. It is wrong for a nation to commit genocide even if its leaders think that doing so would be morally acceptable. Objectively, genocide is evil. (Notice that if we deny the objective evilness of genocide, the whole moral argument against the story of the Amalekites collapses.)

Apologists like Craig agree that genocide is objectively evil, but many of us would go further and say that, whether we use the term "genocide" or not, annihilating a whole society, along with their children, on the basis of something their ancestors did, is objectively evil. Brutally executing children and infants as part of a military campaign is objectively evil. At this point, the apologist has to disagree, because biblical inerrancy requires them to. For my own part, I cannot see the wisdom in this view. Morally, the idea that God would ever command such a thing seems outrageous. It strikes me as intrinsically evil, and quite obviously so.

The inerrantist may challenge us to provide some argument for why annihilating a group of people along with their children and infants should *necessarily* be evil. I do not think we are obligated to provide them with such an argument. Here I am happy to quote Craig again:

> Most of us recognize that sexual abuse of another person is wrong. Actions like rape, torture, child abuse, and brutality aren't just socially unacceptable behavior—they're moral abominations. By the same token, love, generosity, equality, and self-sacrifice are really good. People who fail to see this are just morally handicapped, and there is no reason to allow their impaired vision to call into question what we see clearly.[34]

Craig goes on to suggest that we should be more confident of the reality of objective moral values and duties than of any premise in an argument which denies them. We would thus be irrational to argue ourselves out of believing that torture is objectively evil. Our moral experience provides us with stronger "warrant" (or justification) for believing in objective moral values than any argument could provide for denying them.[35]

In a similar way, I think our perception of the objective evil of brutally killing off an entire society along with its children and infants gives us more warrant than any premise in an argument that such acts can be morally permissible. We do not need an argument to justify our recognition that such actions are evil; we can just "see" that they are. Anyone who fails to see that is, to use Craig's description, "morally handicapped." Just as Craig believes that a good God would not command anyone to torture another person, I believe that a good God would not command anyone to massacre the children of an enemy nation. Since such an act is intrinsically evil, then (given the context) it is entirely appropriate to characterize it as an act of genocide. The only question left for the defender of inerrancy is whether God can command his people to do something horrendously evil for the sake of accomplishing something good.

To say that God was justified in using genocidal actions to destroy his enemies in certain cases is to make one of two claims. Either one must say that there is a possible moral justification for an act as evil as genocide, or one must deny that genocide is intrinsically evil. No one in their right mind can deny that genocide is evil, but let us also recognize the absurdity of suggesting that one could commit genocide in order to accomplish some good. What good would that be? The successful installment of a genocidal government? Apologists like to say that the Amalekites and other pagan societies were completely corrupt, in part, because they participated in child sacrifice. Does it make any sense to massacre children in order to punish a society for slaughtering children?

Defending a Genocidal God

We can quickly dismiss the argument that the Israelites may not have killed children or noncombatants at all. That sounds great, but again, the point here is that God *commanded* them to do it, at least according to the Bible. If that command is morally reprehensible, then the Bible's depiction of God is profoundly misguided.

Some apologists say that the Amalekites "deserved it." It is a shame to have to say this, but nobody deserves to be killed in a genocide. No children or infants deserve to be brutally massacred by an invading army. Any argument to the contrary is rooted in a profoundly disturbing and morally reprehensible worldview. (Regarding the claim that we all deserve such a fate due to our sinful nature, see below.)

Furthermore, to say that the Amalekites deserved their annihilation is to say that the Amalekites, along with their children, were guilty for the sins of their ancestors, since (let's all say it together) that is the only rationale for their destruction provided by God in this passage. We have already shown this to be a direct contradiction of Ezekiel's words, but it also conflicts with our fundamental sense of justice. At this point, I wouldn't care if someone accuses me of being a Western individualist. Anyone who thinks it is okay to kill a child as an act of punishment for anyone's sins (theirs or their parents) has lost touch with their humanity.

As for the idea that God had to utterly annihilate the children of (some of) Israel's enemies so that they would not grow up and fight against Israel or lead them astray with their pagan influence—this is a deeply unpersuasive argument. First of all, the Israelites were already corrupt, at least according to the Bible (see Deuteronomy 9:6-7), so the suggestion that God had to kill the babies of their enemies in order to prevent Israel's corruption is a non-starter. And unless we are prepared to argue that the Amalekite babies were destined by God or genetically predisposed to become so evil as to be beyond redemption (which is theologically and ethically problematic in its own right), there is no reason why it would be impossible for the Israelites to raise the children to live good lives.

The suggestion that Israel did not have the social resources to take care of the children is absurd as a moral justification for their brutal annihilation. If you do not have the resources to take care of your enemy's children, that does not mean it is okay to kill them. If anything, it means that you should probably try to avoid killing your enemy. If you must fight against your enemy in battle, that does not permit you to commit heinous war crimes.

What about the argument that God must be justified in ordering these acts, otherwise he would not be justified in killing people via natural disasters? I suppose an atheist could have a field day here. After all, genocide has no justification. If that means that God is not justified in letting people die in any kind of disaster, then God—or at least, that kind of God—clearly does not exist. That argument might work from an atheist perspective, but for those outside the atheist camp, perhaps there is a better response available.

I would say that, at the very least, there is an important difference between a genocide and an earthquake. The first is a moral act (in the sense that it involves the action of a moral agent, not in the sense that it is good); the second is not. There is also a difference between allowing something to happen and commanding something to happen. Of course, a God who allows genocide to happen is not necessarily less disturbing than a God who commands it to happen. For victims of such crimes, I do not know what comfort there would be in saying, "Actually, God did not *command* this evil thing to happen to you, he only *allowed* it to happen to you." Maybe there is a careful point to be made there. All I am saying is that there is an important moral difference between what you permit and what you demand. Perhaps this offers some hope for the theist. In any case, my point is that this specific argument from the apologist carries no weight, at least not the weight that the apologist thinks it does.

Is it true that we cannot trust our moral intuitions? If so, this would throw us into a state of complete moral agnosticism. (It would also undercut conservative evangelical thinking on a number of social issues.) Either we can recognize certain things as objectively evil or we cannot. If we can, then one is much harder pressed to explain why the act of annihilating a whole society along with their children and infants, particularly as an act of revenge, should not be considered evil.

It is strange when some Christians speak as if God had to have the Israelites commit these brutal acts in order to accomplish his plans for the redemption for all humanity. This is just another way of saying that God had to command evil behavior in order to put an end to evil behavior. It is incoherent, and it is bad theology.

Earlier we considered the problem with saying that the Amalekites "deserved" to be killed, but as we have seen, many inerrantists would say that, actually, we all deserve to be killed, even those who are children, because we all have a sinful nature. Isn't this the natural corollary of the doctrine that all humans are sinners who deserve to spend an eternity in hell? In response, I might say that this just goes to show how morally incoherent the doctrine of hell is. To fully explore that point, a rigorous analysis of the concept of hell would be needed here, but I think there is an easier way to expose the folly of this argument. To say that we all deserve to die as the Amalekites did completely destroys the logic of the earlier point that the Amalekites were slaughtered because they deserved to die. If we all deserve it, and yet by God's grace we are not all subjected to it, then there is no reason why some should suffer such a brutal fate while others do not. Why should special provision be made for the genocide of only some people?

Anytime an inerrantist defends the God of the Old Testament

by saying that everything he did was intended to bring redemption and salvation to all people, I want to add, "Well, except for the Amalekites." On the inerrantist's view, there was something about the Amalekites' national identity such that *every single one of them*, including the poor and destitute ones, and even those who had no control over their nation's leadership, was intrinsically and irredeemably evil. This is a severely broken way of thinking. In fact, it is a genocidal way of thinking.

The Age of Accountability

"But," the apologist says, "the children who were massacred went straight to heaven. They died before the age of accountability. Since they were too young to understand their need for repentance, God did not subject them to eternal damnation." Craig says that "the death of these children was actually their salvation."[36] In response, I would say that the idea of an "age of accountability" is inconsistent with other important aspects of Christian theology, particularly the doctrine of salvation.

Before getting into that, let's be clear on what we're talking about. Evangelicals often speak of salvation in terms of being forgiven for your sins and receiving God's free gift of eternal life; and they often speak of eternal life in terms of going to heaven when you die. Some evangelicals advocate for a more nuanced approach, since the New Testament says less about "going to heaven" (surprisingly little, actually) and more about resurrection and new creation. Even if people go to heaven when they die, the ultimate Christian hope is really about one day being raised from the dead like Jesus was, and participating in God's new creation—a new heaven and earth.[37] For my purposes here, I will retain the language of "going to heaven," simply because it is how evangelicals usually speak of salvation. In this sense, "heaven" broadly refers to the ultimate reward of those who are saved, namely, an everlasting life of eternal comfort and joy in the glorious presence of God.

The idea of an "age of accountability" is rooted in a specific Christian approach to salvation, one which holds that God wants everyone to be saved, and that salvation is given to people based on their free decision to accept it. On this view, the reason some people are damned to an eternity in hell (however that is defined) is because they freely rejected God's salvation. Universalism (the idea that everyone will be saved) is usually rejected as a heresy, since there are places in the New Testament, and particularly in the teachings of Jesus, which seem to rule it out (for example, see Matthew 25:41-46). God's desire is to save everyone, but because he has endowed humans with free will, he respects their free choice and, thus, some people will not be saved.

The problem that comes up in this model of salvation is that some people die before they are old enough to understand their need for salvation. Since God is just, and since it would be unjust to hold a person accountable for failing to accept something that they were never given a chance to understand, then it must be the case that God saves all those who die before they are old enough to freely receive his offer of salvation. This is what they mean when they talk about the age of accountability.

There are Christians who deny that God wants everyone to be saved, just as they deny that salvation is based on a person's response to God. Instead, God selects certain people to be saved prior to creation, and his decision is not based on anything other than his own sovereign choice. On this view, the reason some people are damned to an eternity in hell is simply because they were not chosen by God. Christians who accept this approach to salvation usually do not believe in an age of accountability.[38] This model of salvation suggests that some people were created for the purpose of experiencing everlasting torment. The problem of genocide pales in comparison to such a horrific concept. We can at least credit many evangelical apologists for rejecting such an abhorrent view.

For inerrantists who believe in an age of accountability, there is no doubt that children who die in a brutal genocide will automatically go to heaven. However, this exposes a serious flaw in their thinking about God. Does God want everyone to be saved? Yes. Will every person be saved? No, because they freely rejected God's offer of salvation. Will those who die before reaching an age of accountability be saved? Yes.

Do you see the problem? If children who die in a brutal genocide automatically go to heaven, then it seems that God has a very effective way to make sure that nobody goes to hell: by implementing a universal policy of infanticide. If he kills people as children, then there is no danger of them growing up and rejecting his offer of salvation. If God wants them to be saved, then he must do everything he can to save them. And since God is able to save those who die before the age of accountability, then he has no reason to give them the opportunity to grow up and reject salvation.

So why wouldn't God see to it that every person died before reaching the age of accountability? For that matter, why are evangelicals not willing to take extreme measures, as their God is, in order to ensure the salvation of more people? Why do they not engage in mass infanticide to make sure that the infants don't grow up to reject salvation? In fact, if they believe that life starts as conception, why should they be opposed to abortion? Certainly abortion is not as traumatic as infanticide. Do evangelicals really want people to be saved or not? Even if a policy of mandatory, universal infanticide makes the present life rather unpleasant, on what grounds can an evangelical say that this outweighs the greater good of achieving eternal salvation for all people?

Copan says that infanticide is out of the question because it is a sin and it involves taking an innocent life.[39] Clearly he is missing the point. If it is true that infanticide is evil *even if it sends the infant to heaven*, then there is no use in appealing to the age of accountability in order to defend the infanticide committed against the Amalekites. On the other hand, if infanticide is justified in cases like these (which is exactly what the apologists claim), then the objection loses its force. In that case, they cannot avoid the questions I am raising. Why does God not see to it that everyone dies before they reach a certain age, in order to guarantee their salvation?

To respond that God's purposes do not need to make sense to us, in this context, would be preposterous, because we have already established that the biblical God desires the salvation of all people, and certainly our eternal well-being is more important than our well-being in this life. Anything God does must be aimed at accomplishing what he wants. If God has a path toward saving everyone in this world and does not take it, it cannot be true that he desires the salvation of every person.

Obviously, I do not actually think mandatory infanticide is a good idea. I am making a reductio ad absurdum argument. We do not need a rational argument to explain why a policy of infanticide is bad. Copan is right to see infanticide as evil. Our moral intuitions give us a clear sense that killing children is wrong. But this moral conviction is incompatible with using the idea of an age of accountability to justify infanticide in the Bible. The implication is unavoidable: if children who die go to heaven, then evangelical theology is profoundly incoherent; and if children who die do not go to heaven, then what God commanded the Israelites to do becomes even more horrific and morally detestable. Either way, it is impossible to accept the truth of the narrative in 1 Samuel 15.

No matter how apologists try to justify the Bible's genocides, the result is a morally incoherent view of God. Once we realize that accepting the Bible's inerrancy or infallibility means accepting a rationalization for certain instances of genocide, the whole project of defending these doctrines must be deemed a lost cause by anyone with a shred of moral decency or human empathy.

This particular issue gave me a lot to think about when I was still a Christian. The more I reflected on it, the more uncomfortable I felt going to church on Sunday and publicly worshiping the God depicted in these Bible verses. How could I literally sing the praises of a God who commands genocide and infanticide? The answer cannot be that we measly humans just have to suck it up and give God our praise. If God is morally perfect, then I do not see how God would be honored by being worshiped in this context. A good God would not command people to brutally exterminate children, much less to kill them based on their national identity. The idea is both morally and theologically incoherent. Is it good for us to attribute this behavior to God?

Chapter Twelve

God's Truthfulness

The doctrine of biblical inerrancy (whether that inerrancy extends to everything the Bible says or only to its theological and moral teachings) is grounded in the truthfulness of God. Numbers 23:19 tells us that "God is not a human being, that he should lie." The point is reiterated in Titus 1:2, which says that God "never lies." If God inspired the Bible, such that the Bible's words are God's words, then these words must be true. In this book I have tried to give a comprehensive explanation for why this approach to the Bible must be rejected.

One enormous problem with a doctrine of biblical inerrancy is that it requires us to ignore things that the Bible plainly says, which defeats the purpose of the doctrine in the first place. Nowhere does this become more clear than in the cases we will be considering in this chapter. We saw a moment ago that certain Bible passages proclaim God's truthfulness, but there are other passages which, taken on their own terms, make it clear that God does not always tell the truth.

God's Deceitfulness

In 1 Kings 22, King Ahab of Israel joins forces with the king of Judah to retrieve the fortress at Ramoth-gilead. Before going into battle, they seek the counsel of Ahab's prophets to confirm whether God will support their action. Most of the prophets assure them that victory will be theirs, but one prophet, named Micaiah, says otherwise. He shares a vision of Israel as a flock of sheep, scattered without a shepherd. This is not good news for Ahab. What Micaiah says next is fascinating:

> Therefore hear the word of the LORD: I saw the LORD sitting on his throne, with all the host of heaven standing beside him to the right and to the left of him. And the LORD said, "Who will entice Ahab, so that he may go up and fall at Ramoth-gilead?" Then one said one thing, and another said another, until a spirit came forward and stood before the LORD, saying, "I will entice him." "How?" the LORD asked him. He replied, "I will go out and be a lying spirit in the mouth of all his prophets." Then the LORD said, "You are to entice him, and you shall succeed; go out and do it." So you see, the LORD has put a lying spirit in the mouth of all these your prophets; the LORD has decreed disaster for you. (1 Kings 22:19-23)

The king and his other prophets take offense at Micaiah's message. In response, Micaiah tells Ahab, "If you return in peace, the LORD has not spoken by me." This accords with what is written about prophets elsewhere in the Bible: "If a prophet speaks in the name of the LORD but the thing does not take place or prove true, it is a word that the LORD has not spoken" (Deuteronomy 18:22). Ahab ignores Micaiah's prediction, and ends up being killed in battle, thus vindicating Micaiah's prophetic message.

What seems remarkable about this story is that ultimately, according to the Bible, God is the reason why four hundred prophets misinformed Ahab about his chances of success in battle. The prophets were apparently not actively lying to Ahab. Rather, they were telling Ahab the message which they had been given by a spirit from God. As we learn from Micaiah's vision, that message was false. The problem is obvious: God commissioned a member of his heavenly court to lie to the prophets, for the purpose of deceiving Ahab. It is hard to understand how God could commission someone to lie on his behalf if he himself is incapable of lying. It is even harder to understand if the reason God cannot lie has to do with his perfect goodness. "I can't lie, that is beneath me; one of my employees will do it for me."

Some apologists claim to see no problem here. J. P. Holding says, "It appears that this objection is asserting that the fact that God does not like lying necessarily implies that He could not use this evil for His own ends as a judgment." Since there is allegedly no contradiction involved there, Holding declares triumphantly that "no further discussion is required on this point."[1] Obviously this response is inadequate. Holding is attacking a straw man. The question here is not whether a good God can use the actions of evil people to bring about a good outcome. Rather, the question is how a God who does not lie could ask a spirit to lie for him.

Glenn Miller notes that the word translated in 1 Kings 22:20 as "entice" can also mean "seduce," and from this he draws a bizarre conclusion: "Seduction DOES NOT necessarily include deception."[2] Yes, but surely if a "lying spirit" is involved (as Miller himself observes), it does include deception. That is just what "lying" means.

Miller also claims that God cannot be involved in deception here because otherwise, why would God have had Micaiah reveal the truth to Ahab? That would defeat his whole plan. This argument is appealing to the Bible's integrity in order to prove the Bible's integrity. A skeptic of inerrancy can respond that humans do not always write perfectly coherent stories. There is no avoiding the awkward fact that, regardless of how we explain God's actions, in this particular Bible story God commissions a lying spirit to commit an act of deception. In other words, he is involved in lying.

Apologists have a variety of views regarding the "lying spirit" from Micaiah's vision.[3] Some believe that the lying spirit is actually Satan, or perhaps some other evil spirit.[4] Others seem to acknowledge that the spirit is a member of God's angelic court.[5] And others do not think that Micaiah's vision should be interpreted literally. It is a symbolic vision, not a transcript of an actual proceeding in God's throne room.[6] Of course, if we are still meant to believe that Ahab's prophets were passing along a message they received from a member of God's angelic court, then the problem remains. How could God commission one of his angels to lie for him if he himself is incapable of lying, or unwilling to lie? The remaining options all attempt to get around this problem by suggesting that God did not actually cause or commission the lie. Rather, he used an evil situation to bring about judgment on an evil person.

The passage never identifies the lying spirit as Satan, or even as an evil spirit. He is not described as an "accuser" or "adversary," which is how Satan is identified elsewhere in the Old Testament (Job 1-2; Zechariah 3:1-2), so this interpretation is already a bit strained. But whether we associate the lying spirit with Satan or not, the main problem here is the fact that God is directly asking for someone to be a lying spirit in the mouth of Ahab's prophets. "Who will do this thing for me?" Again, God is commissioning someone to perform an act of deception. If he is commissioning Satan or an evil spirit, it only seems to make the problem worse, because then we have God asking an evil being to help him.

Perhaps this vision should not be treated as a literal report of something that happened in God's throne room, but the logic behind this argument is a bit convoluted since the whole purpose of Micaiah's vision is to explain to Ahab why he should not trust his other prophets. If Micaiah's point was to reveal that Ahab's prophets were not telling the truth, without suggesting that God was the reason for this, then his vision is incredibly misleading. Even if we grant that the vision is not to be taken completely literally, Micaiah ends his speech to Ahab by saying quite clearly, "So you see, the LORD has put a lying spirit in the mouth of all these your prophets." This last statement is not a vision; it is Micaiah's summary of an event that has taken place.

Pretty much every evangelical resource that discusses this passage makes the point that when humans freely rebel against God, he "turns them over" to their sins. In other words, he allows them to be destroyed by their own evil inclinations. According to the Bible, Ahab had no interest in what God really had to say, turning instead to prophets who would tell him whatever he wanted to hear. God simply allowed this situation to reach its logical conclusion. Since Ahab was relying on false prophets, it cost him his life. Ultimately, he was deceived by his own sinfulness.

This sort of thing seems to be echoed in 2 Thessalonians 2:10-12, in which God sends "a powerful delusion" to those who refuse to be saved, "so that all who have not believed the truth but took pleasure in unrighteousness will be condemned." Ahab was evil, and deserved to be punished, and therefore God punished him by allowing him to be overtaken by deception. Isn't this just how God deals with evil people?

There are a couple of problems here. For one thing, regardless of what Ahab personally deserved, we are still left with a God who really can lie, even though other parts of the Bible tell us that he never lies. This is a significant contradiction, and there is no getting away from it. Even worse, the idea that God deceives the wicked, or allows them to be deceived by false prophets, creates an even bigger theological paradox for those who see the Bible as an inspired revelation from God.

Christianity has traditionally viewed all human beings as sinful and wicked, and fully deserving of eternal misery in hell—arguably the worst punishment there is. Jesus says, "No one is good but God alone" (Mark 10:18). And Paul drives this point home in his letter to the Romans:

> There is no one who is righteous, not even one; there is no one who has understanding, there is no one who seeks God. All have turned aside, together they have become worthless; there is no one who shows kindness, there is not even one. (Romans 3:10-12)

I strongly recommend reading through the passage slowly and considering the meaning of each phrase. It is really quite remarkable what Paul says here: *Nobody understands. Nobody seeks God. Everyone is worthless.*

Now suppose that God really does sometimes send (or allow evil spirits to send) deceptive messages to wicked people in order to guarantee their condemnation—even messages delivered through prophets via an act of inspiration. If God is capable of doing something like that, then how could we ever accept the full reliability of a text that he inspired for the purpose of communicating with people who are all utterly sinful and "worthless" in his eyes? Yet to deny that God would ever deceive anybody (or allow anybody to be deceived) in this manner is to deny those biblical passages which indicate otherwise.

God's Fallibility

There are other significant problems related to God's truthfulness in the Bible. It is not just that he deceives people. In some cases, on the Bible's own testimony, God actually makes mistakes.

In 2 Kings 3, the armies of Israel enter a losing battle on God's promise that victory will be theirs. God promises to hand Moab over to Israel through a prophecy which he confirms via a miracle (3:9-20). And when Israel comes against the Moabite forces in battle, everything seems to be going their way. Most of what God promised them comes true. But then, at the last minute, the Moabite king Mesha offers his son as a human sacrifice to his own god. Somehow this turns the battle against Israel, because a "great wrath" comes against them with such force that they need to withdraw from the battle. As a result, God does not actually hand Moab over to Israel, even though this is what he promised to do through his prophet (see 3:21-27). In other words, according to this Bible story, a genuine prophecy from God turns out to be false, and God's promise comes to nothing.

It is clear that apologists are at a loss for what to say here, since so many of them ignore this passage completely. Of those who address it, some claim that the "wrath" that broke out against Israel after Mesha sacrificed his son was the wrath of their own God—that is, Yahweh. According to one resource, "It seems that just when total victory appeared to be in Israel's grasp, God's displeasure with the Ahab dynasty showed itself in some way that caused the Israelite kings to give up the campaign."[7] Obviously, this is just pulling ideas out of thin air. Even other evangelical resources are skeptical of the suggestion that the "wrath" that broke out against Israel was from their own God.[8] After all, God had promised them the victory, and the story does not provide any indication that the armies of Israel were deviating from what God had said. It only attributes their failure to overtake the Moabites to the wrath that broke out as a result of Mesha's child sacrifice.

Other resources explain this as human wrath which broke out against Israel. "Mesha's troops respond to his desperate act with an anger that carries them to victory against the odds."[9] But this still means that God's prophecy has failed. In this case, God's plan is thwarted by human effort—hardly a point in favor of Christian theology, much less biblical inerrancy.

Perhaps the most amusing attempt to avoid this problem is one resource's bold claim that, actually, Israel did win the battle! But then they decided to go home without defeating the king of Moab, because they could not overcome his forces.[10] Of course, this is just silly. If you can't defeat the king's forces in battle, you did not win the battle. Since God had promised to hand Moab over to Israel, the fact that they could not defeat the Moabite king is a major theological problem, one which the Bible never even tries to resolve. On the Bible's own terms, then, it is possible for God to fail, and it is possible for authentic prophecies from God to be false.

If the Bible passages we've discussed here are really telling us the truth, they call God's truthfulness into question. If God can lie or make mistakes, then we have no reason to trust the Bible's teachings *even if it is inspired.* Anyone who believes that God is perfect in both knowledge and goodness must conclude that, in at least some cases, the Bible gets God wrong. As a result, the Bible cannot be an infallible or inerrant source of theological truth.

Concluding Reflections

Before ending the book, I want to say a few things about why I rejected the Bible's divine origin altogether, rather than simply rejecting its inerrancy. In the absence of inerrancy or infallibility, calling the Bible a divine revelation does not seem to add anything to our understanding of what it says. If the authors of the biblical writings have different, conflicting perspectives shaped by their individual contexts and experiences, and if they make false statements ranging from minor historical errors to significant moral and theological falsehoods, then we cannot take any biblical statement for granted.

What does it mean, then, to call these texts a revelation from God? By its very nature, a revelation from God has to be true. To call a book a divine revelation implies that we can trust what it says, but to call a book a divine revelation while admitting that it is riddled with errors seems incoherent to me. It sounds as if what we really mean is that the book merely *contains* a divine revelation.

After I stopped believing in biblical inerrancy, I held onto the belief that the Bible contains the Word of God, while refraining from identifying the Bible itself as the Word of God. For a while, this seemed perfectly sensible to me. I thought about how God could reveal (in some difficult-to-articulate way) a deep truth to a human author who could then write about that divine truth from within their own cultural and intellectual framework. Even though I might come to see problems with that writer's framework, that would not invalidate the divinely revealed insight. With this understanding of the biblical text, I would no longer have to worry about trying to understand every single oddity in the Bible. For example, I could appreciate Paul's different rhetorical strategies for communicating the gospel without necessarily assuming that each strategy was equally enlightening. What mattered most was the divine message.

But the question this raises should be obvious. What is the divine message enshrined in the Bible? I am not asking what the core themes of Christian theology are. That is an easy question to answer. I am asking, if the Bible merely contains the Word of God, but is not itself identical to the Word of God, then how is that Word to be discerned in its pages? How do we know where to draw the line between fallible human perspectives and infallible divine truth?

The more I reflected on these questions, the more they bothered me. Certainly there are things Paul says that are true, no matter what we do with the Bible. For instance, Paul claims to have met James, the brother of Jesus. There is no reason to doubt this, but this is not something that God had to reveal. Furthermore, Paul was arguably a brilliant man. There is no doubt that he was able to develop some fascinating theological ideas by thinking carefully through the relationship between his scriptures, his life with the church, and his understanding of Jesus. But there are lots of authors who are able to construct elaborate models for thinking about life and human experience without being guided by divine inspiration. Their ingenuity does not require them to be infallible; it does not even require them to be right. So if the Bible merely contains a divine revelation, how can we discern the difference between what God revealed to the biblical writer, and what the writer came up with on their own steam? How do we distinguish God's Word from Paul's words?

It is tempting to attribute all the "major" theological teachings of the Bible to God, such as Paul's concept of justification by faith rather than by works of the law. But since we know that the Bible contains significant theological falsehoods, what allows us to point to certain ideas in the Bible and declare that they are revealed to us by God and therefore true? On what grounds can I conclude that justification by faith was God's idea rather than Paul's? If Paul or any other biblical author can make mistakes, even mistakes of a deeply troubling nature, then why assume that any of his ideas were revealed directly to him by God?

This is why I say that the concept of divine inspiration adds nothing to our understanding of the Bible. If we admit that the Bible can contain grievous errors, then we are obligated to be very careful in assessing which parts of the Bible are true and which are false. Inevitably, the Bible's ideas will be measured against our knowledge of the evidence, our ability to reason, and our sense of what is right or wrong. If the Bible says anything that seems profoundly misguided, we can simply disagree with it and move on with our lives. How is this any different from seeing the Bible as a fully human text?

I do not see what sense there is in describing the Bible as a divine revelation. Maybe the authors were writing in response to authentic experiences of God, but their words, perspectives, and theological judgments seem to be their own. In the end, we are still dealing with a book of human insights. If certain parts of those writings really do reflect things that God revealed to the writers, yet we have no way to distinguish these parts from the others except by using our own judgment, then at a practical level it makes no difference whether the Bible is a divine revelation or not.

I am aware that it is logically invalid to argue that, since we cannot know if any parts of the Bible are a divine revelation, then none of its parts are. However, the more we acknowledge the human qualities of the Bible, the more the idea that God inspired certain parts of the Bible seems contrived: "The Bible really is a divine revelation, but it's the sort of divine revelation that you find in a book containing mistakes, contradictions, morally abhorrent teachings, and incoherent theological views." At a certain point, inspiration in the traditional sense becomes implausible, and then I think it is reasonable to be skeptical about the idea. Unless there is a coherent model which allows us to affirm that God guided the human writers even though they could still make serious mistakes in what they wrote (including mistakes about God's nature and about the moral acceptability of certain genocides), it seems sensible to deny the Bible's inspiration is any literal sense.

I find Marcus Borg's comments on this particular issue to be helpful. He writes:

> Why see the question as an either-or choice? Why not see the Bible as *both* divine and human? In my experience, affirming that it is both only compounds the confusion. When the Bible is seen as both divine and human, we have two options. One is to say that it is *all* divine and *all* human. That may sound good, but it leaves us with the dilemma of treating all of scripture as divine revelation. More typically in my experience, affirming that the Bible is both divine and human leads to the attempt to separate the divine parts from the human parts—as if some of it comes from God and some is a human product. The parts that come from God are then given authority, and the others are not. But the parts that we think come from God are normally the parts we see as important, and thus we simply confer divine authority on what matters to us, whether we be conservatives or liberals.[1]

I cannot help but agree with Borg here. If we try to treat the entire Bible as a divine revelation, then we run into all the problems I have been discussing in this book. If we think that it is only partially a divine revelation, then it is far too easy (and tempting) to assume that all the parts I like come from God, whereas all the parts I don't like stem from human error. That is not how a divine revelation is supposed to work. If all I do when reading the Bible is agree with my own ideas, then nothing is being revealed to me.

By trying to identify certain parts of scripture as divine truth, my concern is that I would be treating my own thoughts as God's. So much misery has been caused in the world by people who thought they were exceptional at discerning God's will. I would much rather treat my ideas as mine and Paul's ideas as Paul's.

We saw earlier that there is no compelling, non-circular way to affirm the Bible's full inspiration. Nor do we have an explanation for why a doctrine that pertains to the original writings should apply to the edited versions of those writings that now appear in the Bible. In light of everything we have discussed, it seems very clear to me that calling the Bible a divine revelation is a serious mistake. The only approach to the Bible that holds up to scrutiny is one which acknowledges that it is a fully human text reflecting purely human perspectives. Whether the writers were responding to real encounters with God and whether they have any theological or spiritual insights to share are matters that have to be decided on other grounds.

Notes

*

Introduction

1. Stein, *Studying the Synoptic Gospels*, 49-96.
2. Ibid., 69-71.
3. Ibid., 71-73.
4. Quoted in Strobel, *The Case for the Real Jesus*, 78.
5. Stein, *Studying the Synoptic Gospels*, 57-59.

Chapter One: What Is Biblical Inerrancy?

1. 2 Timothy 3:16.
2. Bowe, "Inspiration," 641.
3. 2 Peter 1:21, New American Standard Bible.
4. Philo, *Who Is the Heir of Divine Things* 259-60.
5. Josephus, *Against Apion* 1.37-38.
6. McKim, *The Westminster Dictionary of Theological Terms*, 32.
7. Ibid., 163.
8. Ibid., 166.
9. Polkinghorne, "Faith in God the Creator," 203.
10. Borg, *Reading the Bible Again for the First Time*, 30-31.
11. Marsden, *Fundamentalism and American Culture*, 55-62.
12. Ibid., 43-123.
13. Ibid., 117.
14. Ibid., 164-70.
15. Ibid., 66-67.
16. Quoted in ibid., 107.
17. Ibid., 122-23.
18. McGrath, *Dawkins' God*, 78.
19. McGrath, *Christian Theology*, 11-12.
20. *Reply to Faustus the Manichaean* 11.5.
21. *Letters* 82.3.
22. See Levine, *The Misunderstood Jew*.
23. Ehrman, *Misquoting Jesus*, 17-20.
24. Metzger, *The Canon of the New Testament*, 109-10.

25. See Revelation 12:9.

26. Kugel, *Traditions of the Bible*, 98-100.

27. Josephus, *Against Apion* 1.38. Bracketed text is from the source.

28. Kugel, *Traditions of the Bible*, 17-18.

29. Quoted in Kugel, *Traditions of the Bible*, 52.

30. *NIV Study Bible*, 14 n. 1:26.

31. *Epistle of Barnabus* 5:5.

32. *ESV Study Bible*, 51 n. 1:26.

33. Sanders, *Judaism*, 521-22.

34. For example, Daniel 12:1-3.

35. Bird, "Inerrancy Is Not Necessary for Evangelicalism Outside the USA," 150.

36. For more on ancient interpretation strategies, see Chapter 4.

Chapter Two: How Do We Know What the Bible Says?

1. Metzger and Ehrman, *The Text of the New Testament*, 24-25.

2. Ibid., 265-68.

3. Common English Bible.

4. New Revised Standard Version.

5. New International Version.

6. Matto, "Why I Am King James Only," under "No Footnotes."

7. Metzger and Ehrman, *The Text of the New Testament*, 3.

8. Ibid., 250-71.

9. Ehrman, *Misquoting Jesus*, 53-55; Metzger and Ehrman, *The Text of the New Testament*, 33.

10. Metzger and Ehrman, *The Text of the New Testament*, 52-134.

11. Ibid., 50.

12. Ehrman, *Misquoting Jesus*, 89.

13. Metzger and Ehrman, *The Text of the New Testament*, 231-39.

14. Ibid., 276-79.

15. Ibid., 50.

16. Law, *The Historical-Critical Method*, 93-94.

17. Ibid., 106-07.

18. Ehrman, *Misquoting Jesus*, 260; Komoszewski, Sawyer, and Wallace, *Reinventing Jesus*, 56-58.

19. Komoszewski, Sawyer, and Wallace, *Reinventing Jesus*, 59-60.

20. Ibid., 60-62.

21. See the preface to the New Revised Standard Version of the Bible.

22. See Grudem, *Systematic Theology*, 85.

23. "Chicago Statement on Biblical Inerrancy," Article X.

24. Ehrman, *Misquoting Jesus.*

25. Ehrman, *Did Jesus Exist?*, 181.

26. Daniels and McElroy, *Can You Trust Just One Bible?*, 119.

27. See Stark, *The Human Faces of God*, 154-59.

28. See Archer, *Encyclopedia of Bible Difficulties*, 178-79.

29. Ankerberg and Weldon, *The Facts on the King James Only Debate*, 12.

30. Ibid., 12-13.

31. Daniels and McElroy, *Can You Trust Just One Bible?*, 109-22; Ruckman, *King James Onlyism Versus Scholarship Onlyism*, 2-3.

32. Licona, *The Resurrection of Jesus*, 62.

33. See Ehrman, *Did Jesus Exist?*, especially 14-19.

34. Van Voorst, "Peter, Gospel of," 1038.

35. See Quarles, "The Gospel of Peter: Does It Contain a Precanonical Resurrection Narrative?"; Strobel, *The Case for the Real Jesus*, 47.

36. Wright, *Jesus and the Victory of God*, 29-35.

37. Licona, *The Resurrection of Jesus*, 65.

38. Ruckman, *King James Onlyism Versus Scholarship Onlyism*, x.

39. Ibid., 15.

40. Daniels and McElroy, *Can You Trust Just One Bible?*, 107.

41. Ankerberg and Weldon, *The Facts on the King James Only Debate*, 7-9.

42. *Translators to the Readers*, 20.

43. Ibid., 37.

44. Ruckman, *Why I Believe the King James Bible Is the Word of God*, 8-9.

Chapter Three: How Do Evangelicals Approach Inerrancy?

1. "Chicago Statement on Biblical Inerrancy," Mohler, "When the Bible Speaks, God Speaks," 34-35; Southwestern Baptist Theological Seminary.

2. See "Chicago Statement on Biblical Inerrancy."

3. Stark, *The Human Faces of God*, xv.

4. For an evangelical critique of dictation theory see Grudem, *Systematic Theology*, 70-71.

5. Evans, *Fabricating Jesus*, 21.

6. Evans, "Did Jesus Predict His Violent Death and Resurrection?," 161.

7. Evans, *Fabricating Jesus*, 31.

8. Evans, *God Speaks.*

9. Merritt, "N.T. Wright on the Bible and why he won't call himself an inerrantist."

10. Wright, *Surprised by Hope*, 53.

11. Wright, *Simply Christian*, 183.

12. Wright, *Simply Christian*, 183.

13. See Habermas and Licona, *The Case for the Resurrection of Jesus*, 44-45.

14. "Fallen asleep" is a euphemism for death.

15. Allison, *The Resurrection of Jesus*, 168.

16. Licona, *The Resurrection of Jesus*, 552.

17. Ibid., 552-53.

18. See Allison, *The Resurrection of Jesus*, 179.

19. See Blomberg, Foreword to *Defining Inerrancy*, loc. 31-129; Geisler, "Licona Articles".

20. Craig, "Resurrection and the Real Jesus," 164-65.

21. Cheney, *The Life of Christ in Stereo*, 189-92.

22. NET Bible, John 2:14 n. 29.

23. Craig, "Is Biblical Inerrancy Defensible?"

24. Strobel, *The Case for Christ*, 42-44, 46.

25. For an example, see Lisle, *The Ultimate Proof of Creation*.

26. For numerous examples, see Dembski and Licona, *Evidence for God*, 51-139.

27. For some examples, see Giberson and Collins, *The Language of Science and Faith*; "Is Evolutionary Creation compatible with biblical inerrancy?"; McGrath, "A rejoinder to Paul Gardner"; McGrath and McGrath, *The Dawkins Delusion*. See also the debate "Is Intelligent Design Viable?" on Craig's Reasonable Faith website.

28. On these two theories, see Archer, *Encyclopedia of Bible Difficulties*, 344; Arndt, Hoerber, and Roehrs, *Bible Difficulties and Seeming Contradictions*, 184; *ESV Study Bible*, 2081-82 n. 1:18; Geisler and Howe, *Big Book of Bible Difficulties*, 361; Haley, *Alleged Discrepancies of the Bible*, 349-50; *NIV Study Bible*, 1897 n. 1:18.

29. Ninow, "Typology," 1341.

30. Holding and Peters, *Defining Inerrancy*, loc. 193.

31. Ibid.

32. See Conrad, "The Fate of Judas: Matthew 27:3-10"; *HarperCollins Study Bible*, 460 n. 17.23.

33. *HarperCollins Study Bible*, 1668-69 n. 1.17.

34. Eusebius, *Church History* 1.7.

35. *NIV Study Bible*, 1769 n. 3:23-38.

36. Archer, *Encyclopedia of Bible Difficulties*, 316; Arndt, Hoerber, and Roehrs, *Bible Difficulties and Seeming Contradictions*; Geisler and Howe, *Big Book of Bible Difficulties*, 385-86;, 170-72; Haley, *Alleged Discrepancies of the Bible*, 325-26.

37. Brown, *Birth of the Messiah*, 503-04.

38. Ibid., 81-84.

39. Arndt, Hoerber, and Roehrs, *Bible Difficulties and Seeming Contradictions*, 170-72.
40. "On the Genealogies of Jesus."
41. *HarperCollins Study Bible*, 565 n. 3.19.
42. Archer, *Encyclopedia of Bible Difficulties*, 216-17; Geisler and Howe, *Big Book of Bible Difficulties*, 201-02; *NIV Study Bible*, 664 n. 3:19.
43. Erhman, *Jesus, Interrupted*, 35-39.

Chapter Four: How Do Inerrantists Interpret the Bible?

1. Law, *The Historical-Critical Method*, 8-10.
2. Ibid., 4.
3. Ibid., 23.
4. The terminology that follows is borrowed from Holding and Peters, *Defining Inerrancy*, chap. 1.
5. Powell, *Fortress Introduction to the Gospels*, 10.
6. Licona, *The Resurrection of Jesus*, 34.
7. Fretheim, "Jonah, Book of," 730; Rashkow, "Esther, Book of," 428-29.
8. Law, *The Historical-Critical Method*, 26. Italics in original.
9. "Allegory," 42.
10. Augustine, *Questions on the Gospels* 2.19.
11. Borg, *Reading the Bible Again for the First Time*, 43.
12. *The Confessions* 12.18, 32.
13. Law, *The Historical-Critical Method*, 27.
14. McKim, *The Westminster Dictionary of Theological Terms*, 135.
15. Quoted in Stark, *Human Faces of God*, 138-39.
16. See McGrath, *Christian Theology*, 11.
17. *Life of Moses* 2.91. Italics in source.
18. *Life of Moses* 2.92.
19. Archer, *Encyclopedia of Bible Difficulties*, 113.
20. Ibid., 114.
21. Geisler and Howe, *Big Book of Bible Difficulties*, 74.
22. See Chapter 11.
23. Kugel, *How to Read the Bible*, 15.

Chapter Five: How Can We Determine a Text's Meaning?

1. Klein, Blomberg, and Hubbard, *Introduction to Biblical Interpretation*, 90.
2. Law, *The Historical-Critical Method*, 15.
3. Ibid., 16.
4. Ibid., 16.

5. Wright, *New Testament and the People of God*, 50ff.

6. DeWitt, *Worldviews*, 31-33.

7. Baltimore Police Department, *Credible Threat*.

8. See Laughland, et. al., "Baltimore: hail of habeas corpus petitions leads to release of riot suspects."

9. Walsh, "Feds says BPD's claim that gangs formed pact to 'take out' officers was 'non-credible.'"

10. I read many firsthand accounts in my own social media feeds.

11. For a discussion of critical realism as a philosophy of science, see Buch-Hansen and Nielsen, *Critical Realism*. For a discussion pertaining specifically to literature, see Wright, *The New Testament and the People of God*, 31-69.

12. Buch-Hansen and Nielsen, *Critical Realism*, 27-29

13. Collins, *Cosmology and Eschatology in Jewish and Christian Apocalypticism*, 3.

14. Ibid.

15. Ibid., 4.

16. 1 Corinthians 13:12, King James Version.

17. Foster, *Freedom of Simplicity*, 59-60.

18. Powell, *Fortress Introduction to the Gospels*, 71.

19. Evans, *Jesus and His World*, 105.

20. Collins, "U.S. Billionaires Got 62 percent Richer During Pandemic. They're Now Up $1.8 Trillion."

21. Buch-Hansen and Nielsen, *Critical Realism*, 3-8.

22. Ibid.

23. Josephus, *The Jewish War* 6.300-09.

24. Savage, "The Kafkaesque Nightmare of Attorney Steven Donziger, a Literal Prisoner of the Chevron Corporation."

25. Malo, "U.S. defends appointment of special prosecutors in Donziger case."

26. Law, *The Historical-Critical Method*, 29.

Chapter Six: Can Inerrancy Be Falsified?

1. Ehrman, Evans, and Stewart, *Can We Trust the Bible on the Historical Jesus?*

2. CSBI, Article XIV.

3. Fischer, *Historians' Fallacies*, 63.

4. See Bird, "Response to R. Albert Mohler Jr.," 69.

5. Craig, "What Price Biblical Inerrancy?"

6. On deductive and inductive arguments, see DeWitt, *Worldviews*, 37-38.

7. Craig, *Reasonable Faith*, 48.

8. Ibid., 43.

9. Ibid., 44.

10. CSBI, Article XVII.

11. Ibid., "A Short Statement," item 3.

12. Geisler and Howe, *Big Book of Bible Difficulties*, 23-24.

13. Ibid., 24.

14. See especially Komoszewski, Sawyer, and Wallace, *Reinventing Jesus*, chaps. 4-8.

15. Wallace, "Inerrancy and the Text of the New Testament," 211-19.

16. Ibid., 219.

17. Grudem, *Systematic Theology*, 68.

18. Ibid.

19. Lewis, *Miracles*, 33.

Chapter Seven: Can Inerrancy Be Justified?

1. See Ehrman, *Forgery and Counterforgery*; Grafton, *Forgers and Critics*.

2. Hill, "Canon of the New Testament," 218-19.

3. "The Bible," The Ethiopian Orthodox Tewahedo Church Faith and Order.

4. Eusebius, *Church History* 3.25.

5. *Church History* 3.24.

6. Metzger, *The Canon of the New Testament*, 75-112.

7. See *ESV Study Bible*, 2453; Eusebius, *The Church History* 7.25.

8. Metzger, *The Canon of the New Testament*, 253.

9. See Matthew 12:1-4; Acts 1:21-26; 1 Corinthians 9:1.

10. Metzger, *The Canon of the New Testament*, 253.

11. Ibid., 251-53.

12. Ibid., 237-39.

13. Ibid.

14. Ibid., 109-10.

15. See Luke 24:44 and the prologue to Sirach.

16. See Sanders, *Paul*, 56-62.

17. Grudem, *Systematic Theology*, 44.

18. Asale, *1 Enoch as Christian Scripture*, 23-61.

19. Grudem, *Systematic Theology*, 44 n. 7.

20. Asale, *1 Enoch as Christian Scripture*, 37.

21. Tertullian, *On the Apparel of Women* 1.3.

22. Ibid., 68-77.

23. Grudem, *Systematic Theology*, 50.

24. See Sanders, *The Historical Figure of Jesus*, 66-73.

25. For in-depth discussions of each, see Ehrman, *Forgery and Counterforgery*, 192-217; 222-29.

26. See Sheler, *Is the Bible True?*, 30; Strobel, *The Case for Christ*, 22.

27. Sanders and Davies, *Studying the Synoptic Gospels*, 5-16, 21-24.

28. For typical scholarly views of authorship see *The HarperCollins Study Bible*, or any number of (non-evangelical) introductory resources for studying the New Testament.

29. For example, see Komoszewski, Sawyer, and Wallace, *Reinventing Jesus*, 138.

30. Haenchen, *John 1*, 11.

31. Eusebius, *The Church History* 3.39.

32. Ibid.

33. Powell, *Fortress Introduction to the Gospels*, 108-09.

34. Sanders and Davies, *Studying the Synoptic Gospels*, 7-12.

35. Irenaeus, *Against Heresies* 3.1.1. His quotations from each Gospel throughout his writings make it clear that he is referring to the same four Gospels used today.

36. Komoszewski, Sawyer, and Wallace, *Reinventing Jesus*, 139.

37. Powell, *Fortress Introduction to the Gospels*, 68-70.

38. See Sanders and Davies, *Studying the Synoptic Gospels*, 11-12.

39. See Strobel, *The Case for Christ*, 22-23.

40. Blomberg, "The New Testament Canon," 234-37.

41. Geisler, "The Canonicity of the New Testament."

42. Komoszewski, Sawyer, and Wallace, *Reinventing Jesus*, 132.

43. For example, see Strobel, *The Case for Christ*, 56-71.

44. Komoszewski, Sawyer, and Wallace, *Reinventing Jesus*, 104-05.

45. Metzger, *The Canon of the New Testament*, 254-57.

46. Ibid., 256.

47. Ibid.

48. Asale, *1 Enoch as Christian Scripture*, 57-61.

49. Metzger, *The Canon of the New Testament*, 211 n. 6.

50. See Kugel, *How to Read the Bible*, 297-316.

51. For example, see *NIV Study Bible*, 4.

52. Geisler and Howe, *Big Book of Bible Difficulties*, 132.

53. Ibid.

54. Sheler, *Is the Bible True?*, 26-27.

55. Brown, *The Gospel According to John XIII-XXI*, 656-57.

56. Ibid., 1057, 1077-79.

57. Brown, *Gospel According to John I-XII*, especially xxi-xxxix; Haenchen, *John 1*, 23-39; Powell, *Fortress Introduction to the Gospels*, 185-86.

58. Strobel, *The Case for Christ*, 24.

59. Sanders, *Paul*, 225-71.

60. Metzger and Ehrman, *The Text of the New Testament*, 273-74.
61. See Daniel Wallace's comments in Strobel, *The Case for the Real Jesus*, 86-87.
62. See Dawkins, *The Greatest Show on Earth*, 273-84.
63. See Stein, *Studying the Synoptic Gospels*.
64. See Evans et al., *The Synoptic Problem*.
65. Wright, *Simply Christian*, 176.

Chapter Eight: Jude and Enoch

1. Collins, *The Apocalyptic Imagination*, 5.
2. *1 Enoch* 1.9. See Isaac, "1 (Ethiopic Apocalypse of) Enoch," 8.
3. See *NIV Study Bible*, 2235 n. 14.
4. Collins, *Apocalyptic Imagination*, 58; Isaac, "1 Ethiopic Apocalypse of) Enoch," 7.
5. See *NIV Study Bible*, xxix. I do not think it's guaranteed that Abraham and Enoch existed, but we are considering the inerrantist's view on its own terms.
6. Geisler and Howe, *Big Book of Bible Difficulties*, 549.
7. *Net Bible*, Jude 1:15 n. 75.
8. See Archer, *Encyclopedia of Bible Difficulties*, 430; Geisler and Howe, *Big Book of Bible Difficulties*, 549; *NIV Study Bible*, 2235 n. 14.
9. Isaac, "1 (Ethiopic Apocalypse of) Enoch," 6.
10. See Brown, *The Birth of the Messiah*, 208-09.
11. Isaac, "1 (Ethiopic Apocalypse of) Enoch," 6.
12. Asale, *1 Enoch as Christian Scripture*, 32.
13. See Isaac, "1 (Ethiopic Apocalypse of) Enoch," 5-12. See also Collins, *Apocalyptic Imagination*.
14. See Chapter 2.

Chapter Nine: The Field of Blood

1. See *ESV Study Bible*, 1884 n. 27:7-8.
2. Akin, "How Did the Field of Blood Get Its Name?"
3. Holding, "The Death of Judas Iscariot."
4. Bullinger, "The Purchase of 'The Potter's Field.'"
5. Holding, "The Death of Judas Iscariot."
6. Ibid.
7. Wang, "Dubious, curious Arizona place names."
8. Evans, *Jesus and His World*, 21.
9. Powell, *Fortress Introduction to the Gospels*, 66.
10. Paffenroth, "Akeldama."

Chapter Ten: God's Name

1. Lewis, "Hebrew, Biblical," 565-66.
2. McLaughlin, "Yahweh," 1402.
3. "Jehovah," 682.
4. For examples see Archer, *Encyclopedia of Bible Difficulties*, 66-67; Haley, *Alleged Discrepancies of the Bible*, 421; *ESV Study Bible*, 153 n. 6:3-8; Miller, "When was the name 'YAHWEH' revealed?"; NET Bible, Exodus 6:3 n. 9; *NIV Study Bible*, 109-10 n. 6:3.
5. McLaughlin, "Yahweh," 1402.
6. For examples, see *ESV Study Bible*, 2020 n. 1:16-17; Net Bible, John 1:18 n. 48.
7. For example, see Wright, *Simply Christian*, 68.
8. Haley, *Alleged Discrepancies of the Bible*, 421.
9. Geisler and Howe, *Big Book of Bible Difficulties*, 68-69.

Chapter Eleven: Revenge on the Amalekites

1. See Arndt, Hoerber, and Roehrs, *Bible Difficulties and Seeming Contradictions*, 221; Geisler and Howe, *Big Book of Bible Difficulties*, 285.
2. Holding, "Sins of the Fathers in the Bible."
3. Geisler and Howe, *Big Book of Bible Difficulties*, 285.
4. Arndt, Hoerber, and Roehrs, *Bible Difficulties and Seeming Contradictions*, 221.
5. See Craig, "The 'Slaughter' of the Canaanites Re-visited"; Miller, "Shouldn't the butchering of the Amalekite children be considered war crimes?"
6. See Craig, "Slaughter of the Canaanites."
7. See Copan, *Is God a Moral Monster?*, 173-75; Craig, "The 'Slaughter' of the Canaanites Re-visited."
8. Geisler and Howe, *Big Book of Bible Difficulties*, 161.
9. Craig, "Slaughter of the Canaanites."
10. Haley, *Alleged Discrepancies of the Bible*, 94.
11. Copan, *Is God a Moral Monster?*, 159.
12. See *ESV Study Bible*, 515 n. 15:3; Geisler and Howe, *Big Book of Bible Difficulties*, 161.
13. Craig, "Slaughter of the Canaanites."
14. See Geisler and Howe, *Big Book of Bible Difficulties*, 161; Haley, *Alleged Discrepancies of the Bible*, 94.
15. See Miller, "Shouldn't the butchering of the Amalekite children be considered war crimes?" The childbirth example is Miller's.
16. See Baggett and Walls, *Good God*, 139; Copan, *Is God a Moral Monster?*, 166.
17. Geisler and Howe, *Big Book of Bible Difficulties*, 161.
18. Baggett and Walls, *Good God*, 138-39.

19. Miller, "Shouldn't the butchering of the Amalekite children be considered war crimes?"

20. See Craig, "Slaughter of the Canaanites"; Geisler and Howe, *Big Book of Bible Difficulties*, 161.

21. Jones, *Genocide*, 14-17.

22. Miller, "Shouldn't the butchering of the Amalekite children be considered war crimes?"

23. Jones, *Genocide*, 15.

24. Ibid., 15, 19-20.

25. Ibid., 23-27.

26. Ibid., 25.

27. Ibid.

28. Naimark, *Genocide*, 34-47.

29. Miller, "Shouldn't the butchering of the Amalekite children be considered war crimes?"

30. Naimark, *Genocide*, 340-41.

31. See Jones, *Genocide*, 6-7; Naimark, *Genocide*, 8-9.

32. Craig, *Reasonable Faith*, 179.

33. Ibid., 172.

34. Ibid., 181.

35. Ibid.

36. Craig, "Slaughter of the Canaanites."

37. See Wright, *Surprised by Hope*.

38. For an example of someone who takes these positions, see Grudem, *Systematic Theology*, 629, 641, 816-37.

39. Copan, *Is God a Moral Monster?*, 194.

Chapter Twelve: God's Truthfulness

1. Holding, "Why did God use lying spirits?"

2. Miller, "How can God not lie and still Deceive the Wicked?" Original formatting preserved.

3. *NIV Study Bible*, 587 n. 22:23.

4. See Arndt, Hoerber, and Roehrs, *Bible Difficulties and Seeming Contradictions*, 55.

5. See Archer, *Encyclopedia of Bible Difficulties*, 410

6. See Geisler and Howe, *Big Book of Bible Difficulties*, 188-89; Haley, *Alleged Discrepancies of the Bible*, 98.

7. *NIV Study Bible*, 597 n. 3:27.

8. See NET Bible, 2 Kings 3:27 n. 43.

9. *ESV Study Bible*, 651 n. 3:27.
10. See NET Bible, 2 Kings 3:27, "Constable's Notes."

Concluding Reflections

1. Borg, *Reading the Bible Again for the First Time*, 26-27.

Bibliography

Achtemeier, Paul J. *1 Peter: A Commentary on First Peter*. Edited by Eldon Jay Epp. Hermeneia – A Critical and Historical Commentary on the Bible. Minneapolis: Fortress Press, 1996.

Akin, Jimmy. "How Did the Field of Blood Get Its Name?" Catholic Answers Shop Blog. March 23, 2021. https://shop.catholic.com/blog/how-did-the-field-of-blood-get-its-name.

"Allegory." In *Eerdmans Dictionary of the Bible*, edited by David Noel Freedman, Allen C. Myers, and Astrid B. Beck. Grand Rapids: William B Eerdmans Publishing Company, 2000.

Allison, Dale C., Jr. *The Resurrection of Jesus: Apologetics, Polemics, History*. New York: Bloomsbury, 2021.

Ankerberg, John and John Weldon. *The Facts on the King James Only Debate*. ATRI Publishing, 2011. Kindle e-book.

Archer, Gleason L. *Encyclopedia of Bible Difficulties*. Grand Rapids: Zondervan, 1982.

Arndt, William, Robert G. Hoerber, and Walter R. Roehrs. *Bible Difficulties and Seeming Contradictions*. St. Louis: Concordia Publishing House, 1987.

Asale, Bruk Ayele. *1 Enoch as Christian Scripture: A Study in the Reception and Appropriation of 1 Enoch in Jude and the Ethiopian Orthodox Tewahedo Canon*. Eugene, OR: Pickwick Publications, 2020.

Attridge, Harold W. et al., editors. *The HarperCollins Study Bible, Revised Edition*. San Francisco: HarperOne, 2006.

Augustine. *The Confessions of Saint Augustine*. Translated by J. G. Pilkington. The Complete Works of Saint Augustine. 2019. Kindle e-book.

Augustine. *Letters of Saint Augustine*. Edited by Philip Schaff. Translated by John George Cunningham. The Complete Works of Saint Augustine. 2019. Kindle e-book.

Augustine. *Questions on the Gospels*. Edited by John Litteral. Litteral Truth Publishing. Kindle e-book.

Augustine. *Reply to Faustus the Manichaean*. Edited by Philip Schaff.

Translated by Rev. Richard Stothert. *The Complete Works of Saint Augustine.* 2019. Kindle e-book.

Baggett, David, and Jerry L. Walls. *Good God: The Theistic Foundations of Morality.* Oxford: Oxford University Press, 2011.

Baltimore Police Department Office of the Police Commissioner Media Relations Section, 2015. *Credible Threat to Law Enforcement.* [online] Available at: <https://www.scribd.com/doc/263262264/Credible-Threat> [Accessed 9 November 2021].

Barker, Kenneth L. et al., eds. *NIV Study Bible: Fully Revised Edition.* Grand Rapids: Zondervan, 2020.

"The Bible." The Ethiopian Orthodox Tewahedo Church Faith and Order. Accessed November 9, 2021. https://ethiopianorthodox.org/english/canonical/books.html.

Bird, Michael F. "Inerrancy Is Not Necessary for Evangelicalism Outside the USA." In *Five Views on Biblical Inerrancy*, edited by J. Merrick, Stephen M. Garrett, and Stanley N. Gundry, 145-73. Grand Rapids: Zondervan, 2013.

Bird, Michael F. "Response to R. Albert Mohler, Jr." In *Five Views on Biblical Inerrancy*, edited by J. Merrick, Stephen M. Garrett, and Stanley N. Gundry, 65-70. Grand Rapids: Zondervan, 2013.

Blomberg, Craig L. Foreword to *Defining Inerrancy: Affirming a Defensible Faith for a New Generation*, by J. P. Holding and Nick Peters, loc. 31-129. Tekton Apologetics Ministries, 2014. Kindle e-book.

Blomberg, Craig L. "The New Testament Canon." In *Evidence for God: 50 Arguments for Faith from the Bible, History, Philosophy, and Science*, edited by William A. Dembski and Michael R. Licona, 234-37. Baker Books, 2010, pp.234-37.

Boice, James Montgomery. *Does Inerrancy Matter?* Oakland: International Council on Biblical Inerrancy, 1979.

Borg, Marcus J. Reading the Bible Again for the First Time: Taking the Bible Seriously But Not Literally. San Francisco: HarperSanFrancisco, 2002.

Bowe, Barbara E. "Inspiration." In *Eerdmans Dictionary of the Bible*, edited by David Noel Freedman, Allen C. Myers, and Astrid B. Beck. Grand Rapids: William B Eerdmans Publishing Company, 2000.

Brown, Raymond E. *The Birth of the Messiah: A Commentary on the Infancy Narratives in Matthew and Luke.* Garden City, NY: Image Books, 1979.

Brown, Raymond E. *The Gospel According to John I-XII: A New Translation with Introduction and Commentary.* The Anchor Yale Bible. Vol 29. New Haven: Yale University Press, 2008.

Brown, Raymond E. *The Gospel According to John XIII-XXI: A New Translation with Introduction and Commentary.* The Anchor Yale Bible. Vol. 29A. New Haven: Yale University Press, 2008.

Buch-Hansen, Hubert, and Peter Nielsen. *Critical Realism: Basics and Beyond.* London: Red Globe Press, 2020. Kindle e-book.

Bullinger, E. W. "'The Purchase of The Potters Field' (Matthew 27:6-8, and Acts 1:18, 19) and the Fulfilment of the Prophecy (Matthew 27:9, 10)." The Companion Bible. Accessed November 9, 2021. https://www.companionbiblecondensed.com/AP/ap161/index.html?page=1.

Cheney, Johnston M. *The Life of Christ in Stereo: The Four Gospels Combined as One.* 2nd ed. Portland: Western Baptist Seminary Press, 1971.

"Chicago Statement on Biblical Inerrancy." Southwestern Baptist Theological Seminary. Accessed November 9, 2021. https://swbts.edu/affirmed-statements/chicago-statement.

Collins, Adela Yarbro. *Cosmology and Eschatology in Jewish and Christian Apocalypticism.* Leiden, The Netherlands: Brill, 2000.

Collins, Chuck. "U.S. Billionaires Got 62 percent Richer During Pandemic. They're Now Up $1.8 Trillion." *Institute for Policy Studies.* August 24, 2021. https://ips-dc.org/u-s-billionaires-62-percent-richer-during-pandemic.

Collins, Francis S. *The Language of God: A Scientist Presents Evidence for Belief.* New York: Free Press, 2006.

Collins, John J. *The Apocalyptic Imagination: An Introduction to Jewish Apocalyptic Literature.* 3rd ed. Grand Rapids: William B. Eerdmans Publishing Company, 2016.

Collins, John J. *Daniel: A Commentary on the Book of Daniel.* Edited by Frank Moore Cross. Hermeneia – A Critical and Historical Commentary on the Bible. Minneapolis: Fortress Press, 1993.

Conrad, Audrey. "The Fate of Judas: Matthew 27:3-10." *Toronto Journal of Theology* 7, no. 2 (September 1991): 158-68. https://www.utpjournals.press/doi/abs/10.3138/tjt.7.2.158.

Coogan, Michael D. et al., eds. *The New Oxford Annotated Bible with Apocrypha: New Revised Standard Version.* 4th ed. Oxford: Oxford University Press, 2010.

Copan, Paul. *Is God a Moral Monster? Making Sense of the Old Testament God.* Grand Rapids: Baker Books, 2011.

Copi, Irving M. *Introduction to Logic.* 7th ed. New York: MacMillan Publishing Company, 1986.

Craig, William Lane. "Is Biblical Inerrancy Defensible?" Reasonable Faith. November 22, 2020. https://www.reasonablefaith.org/writings/question-answer/is-biblical-inerrancy-defensible.

Craig, William Lane. *Reasonable Faith: Christian Truth and Apologetics.* 3rd ed. Wheaton: Crossway, 2008.

Craig, William Lane. "Resurrection and the Real Jesus." In *Will the Real Jesus Please Stand Up? A Debate between William Lane Craig and John Dominic Crossan.* Edited by Paul Copan. Grand Rapids: Baker Books, 1998.

Craig, William Lane. "Slaughter of the Canaanites." Reasonable Faith. August 6, 2007. https://www.reasonablefaith.org/writings/question-answer/slaughter-of-the-canaanites.

Craig, William Lane. "The 'Slaughter' of the Canaanites Re-visited." Reasonable Faith. August 8, 2011. https://www.reasonablefaith.org/writings/question-answer/the-slaughter-of-the-canaanites-re-visited.

Craig, William Lane. "What Price Biblical Inerrancy?" Reasonable Faith. July 2, 2007. https://www.reasonablefaith.org/question-answer/P20/what-price-biblical-errancy.

Croy, N. Clayton. *The Mutilation of Mark's Gospel.* Nashville: Abingdon Press, 2003.

Daniels, David W., and Jack McElroy. *Can You Trust Just One Bible?* Ontario, CA: Chick Publications, 2015.

Dawkins, Richard. *The Greatest Show on Earth: The Evidence for Evolution.* New York: Free Press, 2009.

Dembski, William A., and Michael R. Licona, eds. *Evidence for God: 50 Arguments for Faith from the Bible, History, Philosophy, and Science.* Grand Rapids: Baker Books, 2010.

Dennis, Lane T. et al., eds. *ESV Study Bible.* Wheaton: Crossway, 2016.

"Deuterocanonical Books." In *Eerdmans Dictionary of the Bible*, edited by David Noel Freedman, Allen C. Myers, and Astrid B. Beck. Grand Rapids: William B Eerdmans Publishing Company, 2000.

DeWitt, Richard. *Worldviews: An Introduction to the History and Philosophy of Science.* 3rd ed. Hoboken, NJ: Wiley Blackwell, 2018.

Ehrman, Bart D. *Did Jesus Exist? The Historical Argument for Jesus of Nazareth.* New York: HarperOne, 2012.

Ehrman, Bart D. *Forgery and Counterforgery: The Use of Literary Deceit in Early Christian Polemics.* Oxford: Oxford University Press, 2013.

Ehrman, Bart D. *Jesus, Interrupted: Revealing the Hidden Contradictions in the Bible (and Why We Don't Know About Them)*. New York: HarperOne, 2010.

Ehrman, Bart D. *Lost Christianities: The Battles for Scripture and the Faiths We Never Knew*. Oxford: Oxford University Press, 2005.

Ehrman, Bart D. *Lost Scriptures: Books that Did Not Make It into the New Testament*. Oxford: Oxford University Press, 2005.

Ehrman, Bart D. *Misquoting Jesus: The Story Behind Who Changed the Bible and Why*. New York: HarperOne, 2005. PLUS paperback.

Ehrman, Bart D., Craig A. Evans, and Robert B. Stewart. *Can We Trust the Bible on the Historical Jesus?* Louisville, KY: Westminster John Knox Press, 2020.

Enoch, Book of. Edited by James H. Charlesworth. Translated by E. Isaac. The Old Testament Pseudepigrapha: Volume One: Apocalyptic Literature and Testaments. Peabody, MA: Hendrickson Publishers, 1983.

The Epistle of Barnabus. Edited by Betty Radick. Translated by Maxwell Staniforth and Andrew Louth. Early Christian Writings: The Apostolic Fathers. London: Penguin Books, 1987.

Eusebius. *The Church History*. Translated by Paul L. Maier. Grand Rapids: Kregel Academic & Professional, 2007.

Evans, Craig A. "Did Jesus Predict His Violent Death and Resurrection?" In *Evidence for God: 50 Arguments for Faith from the Bible, History, Philosophy, and Science*, edited by William A. Dembski and Michael R. Licona, 160-63. Grand Rapids: Baker Books, 2010.

Evans, Craig A. *Fabricating Jesus: How Modern Scholars Distort the Gospels*. Downers Grove, IL: IVP Books, 2006.

Evans, Craig A. *God Speaks: What He Says, What He Means*. Franklin, TN: Worthy Publishing, 2015.

Evans, Craig A. *Jesus and His World: The Archaeological Evidence*. Louisville, KY: Westminster John Knox Press, 2013.

Evans, Craig A. et al. *The Synoptic Problem: Four Views*. Edited by Stanley E. Porter and Bryan R. Dyer. Grand Rapids: Baker Academic, 2016.

Fairchild, Mark R. "Star." In *Eerdmans Dictionary of the Bible*, edited by David Noel Freedman, Allen C. Myers, and Astrid B. Beck. Grand Rapids: William B Eerdmans Publishing Company, 2000.

Fee, Gordon D. *The First Epistle to the Corinthians*. The New International Commentary on the New Testament. Grand Rapids: William B. Eerdmans Publishing Company, 1987.

Fischer, David Hackett. *Historians' Fallacies: Toward a Logic of Historical Thought*. New York: HarperPerennial, 1970.

Foster, Richard J. *Freedom of Simplicity: Finding Harmony in a Complex World – Revised and Updated*. New York: HarperOne, 2005.

Fretheim, Terence E. "Jonah, Book of." In *Eerdmans Dictionary of the Bible*, edited by David Noel Freedman, Allen C. Myers, and Astrid B. Beck. Grand Rapids: William B Eerdmans Publishing Company, 2000.

Geisler, Norman. "The Canonicity of the New Testament." Pinpoint Evangelism. Accessed November 9, 2021. http://www.pinpointevangelism.com/The-Canonicity-of-the-Bible.pdf.

Geisler, Norman. "Licona Articles." Norman Geisler. Accessed November 9, 2021. http://normangeisler.com/licona-articles.

Geisler, Norman L., and Thomas Howe. *The Big Book of Bible Difficulties: Clear and Concise Answers from Genesis to Revelation*. Grand Rapids: Baker Books, 1992.

Giberson, Karl W., and Francis S. Collins. *The Language of Science and Faith: Straight Answers to Genuine Questions*. Downers Grove, IL: IVP Books, 2011.

Grafton, Anthony. *Forgers and Critics, New Edition: Creativity and Duplicity in Western Scholarship*. Princeton: Princeton University Press, 2019.

Gregory of Nyssa. *The Life of Moses*. Translated by Abraham J. Malherbe and Everett Ferguson. New Humanity Institute. Accessed November 9, 2021. http://www.newhumanityinstitute.org/pdf-articles/Gregory-of-Nyssa-The-Life-of-Moses.pdf.

Grudem, Wayne. *Systematic Theology: An Introduction to Biblical Doctrine*. 2nd ed. Grand Rapids: Zondervan Academic, 2020.

Habermas, Gary R., and Michael Licona. *The Case for the Resurrection of Jesus*. Grand Rapids: Kregel Publications, 2004.

Haenchen, Ernst. *John 1: A Commentary on the Gospel of John Chapters 1-6*. Edited by Robert W. Funk and Ulrich Busse. Translated by Robert W. Funk. Hermeneia – A Critical and Historical Commentary on the New Testament. Philadelphia: Fortress Press, 1984.

Haley, John W. *Alleged Discrepancies of the Bible*. Grand Rapids: Baker Book House, 1988.

Hill, Charles E. "Canon of the New Testament." In *Eerdmans Dictionary of the Bible*, edited by David Noel Freedman, Allen C. Myers, and Astrid B. Beck. Grand Rapids: William B Eerdmans Publishing Company, 2000.

Holding, J. P. "The claim is made that Abiathar was not high priest. . .

." Tekton Apologetics. Accessed November 9, 2021. https://www.tek-tonics.org/tsr/abby.php.

Holding, J. P. "By some Skeptics' thinking, Jeremiah 7:22. . . ." Tekton Apologetics. Accessed November 9, 2021. https://www.tektonics.org/tsr/jerry722.php#fig.

Holding, J. P. "On the Genealogies of Jesus." Tekton Apologetics. Accessed November 9, 2021. https://www.tektonics.org/gk/jesgen.php.

Holding, J. P. "Sins of the Fathers in the Bible." Tekton Apologetics. Accessed November 9, 2021. http://www.tektonics.org/lp/paydaddy.php.

Holding, J. P. "Why did God use lying spirits?" Tekton Apologetics. Accessed November 9, 2021. http://www.tektonics.org/lp/lying-ghosts.php.

Holding, J. P., and Nick Peters. *Defining Inerrancy: Affirming a Defensible Faith for a New Generation.* Tekton Apologetics Ministries, 2014. Kindle e-book.

Irenaeus. *Against Heresies.* Translated by Alexander Roberts and W. H. Rambaut. The Writings of Irenaeus. Edinburgh: Aeterna Press, 2015.

"Is Evolutionary Creation compatible with biblical inerrancy?" BioLogos. February 18, 2020. https://biologos.org/common-questions/is-evolutionary-creation-compatible-with-biblical-inerrancy.

Isaac, E. "1 (Ethiopic Apocalypse of) Enoch (Second Century B.C.-First Century A.D.)." In *The Old Testament Pseudepigrapha, Volume One: Apocalyptic Literature and Testaments,* edited by James H. Charlesworth, 5-90. Peabody, MA: Hendrickson Publishers, 1983.

"Jehovah." In *Eerdmans Dictionary of the Bible,* edited by David Noel Freedman, Allen C. Myers, and Astrid B. Beck. Grand Rapids: William B Eerdmans Publishing Company, 2000.

Jones, Adam. *Genocide: A Comprehensive Introduction.* 3rd ed. London: Routledge, 2017.

Josephus, Flavius. *Against Apion.* Translated by William Whiston. The New Complete Works of Josephus: Revised and Expanded Edition. Grand Rapids: Kregel Publications, 1999.

Josephus, Flavius. *The Jewish War.* Translated by William Whiston. The New Complete Works of Josephus: Revised and Expanded Edition. Grand Rapids: Kregel Publications, 1999.

Keck, Leander E., and J. Louis Martyn. *Studies in Luke-Acts.* Nashville: Abingdon Press, 1966.

Klein, William W., Craig L. Blomberg, and Robert L. Hubbard. *Introduction to Biblical Interpretation.* Nashville: W Publishing Group, 1993.

Komoszewski, J. Ed, M. James Sawyer, and Daniel B. Wallace. *Reinventing Jesus: How Contemporary Skeptics Miss the Real Jesus and Mislead Popular Culture*. Grand Rapids: Kregel Publications, 2006.

Kugel, James L. *How to Read the Bible: A Guide to Scripture, Then and Now*. New York: Free Press, 2007.

Kugel, James L. *Traditions of the Bible: A Guide to the Bible as It Was at the Start of the Common Era*. Cambridge, MA: Harvard University Press, 1998.

Laughland, Oliver, et. al. "Baltimore: hail of habeas corpus petitions leads to release of riot suspects." *The Guardian*. April 30, 2015. https://www.theguardian.com/us-news/2015/apr/30/baltimore-hail-of-habeas-corpus-petitions-leads-to-release-of-riot-suspects.

Law, David R. *The Historical-Critical Method: A Guide for the Perplexed*. London: Bloomsbury T&T Clark, 2012. Kindle e-book.

Levine, Amy-Jill. *The Misunderstood Jew: The Church and the Scandal of the Jewish Jesus*. New York: HarperOne, 2006.

Lewis, C. S. *Miracles*. San Francisco: HarperSanFrancisco, 2001.

Lewis, Theodore J. "Hebrew, Biblical." In *Eerdmans Dictionary of the Bible*, edited by David Noel Freedman, Allen C. Myers, and Astrid B. Beck. Grand Rapids: William B Eerdmans Publishing Company, 2000.

Licona, Michael R. *The Resurrection of Jesus: A New Historiographical Approach*. Downers Grove, IL: IVP Academic, 2010.

Lisle, Jason. *The Ultimate Proof of Creation: Resolving the Origins Debate*. Green Forest, AR: Master Books, 2009.

Malo, Sebastien. "U.S. defends appointment of special prosecutors in Donziger case." *Reuters*. November 12, 2021. https://www.reuters.com/legal/litigation/us-defends-appointment-special-prosecutors-donziger-case-2021-11-13.

Marsden, George M. *Fundamentalism and American Culture*. 2nd ed. Oxford: Oxford University Press, 2006.

Matto, Ken. "Why I Am King James Only." Scion of Zion. Accessed November 11, 2021. https://www.scionofzion.com/kjo.htm.

McDowell, Josh and Sean McDowell. *Evidence that Demands a Verdict: Life-Changing Truth for a Skeptical World*. Nashville: Thomas Nelson, 2017.

McGrath, Alister E. *Christian Theology: An Introduction*. 6th ed. West Sussex, UK: Wiley Blackwell, 2017.

McGrath, Alister E. *Dawkins' God: Genes, Memes, and the Meaning of Life*. Malden, MA: Blackwell Publishing, 2005.

McGrath, Alister E. "A rejoinder to Paul Gardner." Evangelicals Now. Accessed November 9, 2021. https://www.e-n.org.uk/1997/01/features/a-rejoinder-to-paul-gardner.

McGrath, Alister E., and Joanna Collicutt McGrath. *The Dawkins Delusion? Atheist Fundamentalism and the Denial of the Divine.* Downers Grove, IL: IVP Books, 2007.

McKim, Donald K. *The Westminster Dictionary of Theological Terms.* 2nd ed. Louisville, KY: Westminster John Knox Press, 2014. Kindle e-book.

McLaughlin, John L. "Yahweh." In *Eerdmans Dictionary of the Bible*, edited by David Noel Freedman, Allen C. Myers, and Astrid B. Beck. Grand Rapids: William B Eerdmans Publishing Company, 2000.

Merritt, Jonathan, "N.T. Wright on the Bible and why he won't call himself an inerrantist." Religion News Service. June 2, 2014. https://religionnews.com/2014/06/02/n-t-wright-bible-isnt-inerrantist.

Metzger, Bruce M. *The Canon of the New Testament: Its Origin, Development, and Significance.* Oxford: Clarendon Press, 1987.

Metzger, Bruce M., and Bart D. Ehrman. *The Text of the New Testament: Its Transmission, Corruption, and Restoration.* 4th ed. Oxford: Oxford University Press, 2005.

Miller, Glenn. "Did the Jews understand the 'weeks' of Daniel to refer to 'years'?" March 28, 1998. Christian ThinkTank. https://www.christian-thinktank.com/q70weeks.html.

Miller, Glenn. "How can God not lie and still Deceive the Wicked?" Christian ThinkTank. June 3, 1996. https://www.christian-think-tank.com/godlies.html.

Miller, Glenn. "Shouldn't the butchering of the Amalekite children be considered war crimes?" Christian ThinkTank. Accessed November 9, 2021. https://www.christianthinktank.com/rbutcher1.html.

Miller, Glenn. "Was God being evil when He killed all the firstborn in Egypt?" Christian ThinkTank. Accessed November 9, 2021. https://www.christian-thinktank.com/killheir.html.

Miller, J. Maxwell and John H Hayes. *A History of Ancient Israel and Judah.* 2nd ed. Louisville, KY: Westminster John Knox Press, 2006.

Mohler, R Albert, Jr. "When the Bible Speaks, God Speaks." *Five Views on Biblical Inerrancy*, edited by J. Merrick, Stephen M. Garrett, and Stanley N. Gundry, 29-58. Grand Rapids: Zondervan, 2013.

Naimark, Norman M. *Genocide: A World History.* Oxford: Oxford University Press, 2017.

NET (New English Translation) Bible. Accessed November 9, 2021. https://netbible.org/bible.

Neyrey, Jerome H. *2 Peter, Jude: A New Translation with Introduction and Commentary*. The Anchor Bible. Vol. 37C. New Haven: Yale University Press, 1993.

Ninow, Friedbert. "Typology." In *Eerdmans Dictionary of the Bible*, edited by David Noel Freedman, Allen C. Myers, and Astrid B. Beck. Grand Rapids: William B Eerdmans Publishing Company, 2000.

Osborn, Ronald E. *Death Before the Fall: Biblical Literalism and the Problem of Animal Suffering*. Downers Grove, IL: IVP Academic, 2014.

Paffenroth, Kim. "Akeldama." In *Eerdmans Dictionary of the Bible*, edited by David Noel Freedman, Allen C. Myers, and Astrid B. Beck. Grand Rapids: William B Eerdmans Publishing Company, 2000.

Philo of Alexandria. *Who Is the Heir of Divine Things*. Translated by C. D. Yonge. The Works of Philo: Complete and Unabridged – New Updated Version. Peabody, MA: Hendrickson Publishers, 2018.

Piepkorn, Arthur Carl. "What Does 'Inerrancy' Mean?" *Concordia Theological Monthly* 39, no. 8 (Sep. 1965): 577-93. https://lutherantheology.files.wordpress.com/2010/12/piepkorn-inerrancy.pdf.

Polkinghorne, John. "Faith in God the Creator." In *Belief: Readings on the Reason for Faith*, edited by Francis Collins, 198-215. New York: HarperOne, 2010.

Powell, Mark Allan. *Fortress Introduction to the Gospels*. 2nd ed. Minneapolis: Fortress Press, 2019.

Quarles, Charles L. "The Gospel of Peter: Does It Contain a Preconcanical Resurrection Narrative?" In *The Resurrection of Jesus: John Dominic Crossan and N. T. Wright in Dialogue*, edited by Robert B. Stewart, 106-20. Minneapolis: Fortress Press, 2006.

Rashkow, Ilona N. "Esther, Book of." In *Eerdmans Dictionary of the Bible*, edited by David Noel Freedman, Allen C. Myers, and Astrid B. Beck. Grand Rapids: William B Eerdmans Publishing Company, 2000.

Robinson, James M. et al., eds. *The Sayings Gospel Q in Greek and English with Parallels from the Gospels of Mark and Thomas*. Minneapolis: Fortress Press, 2002.

Ruckman, Peter S. *King James Onlyism Versus Scholarship Onlyism*. Pensacola, FL: BB Bookstore, 1992.

Ruckman, Peter S. *Why I Believe the King James Bible is the Word of God*. Pensacola, FL: BB Bookstore, 1983.

Sanders, E. P. *The Historical Figure of Jesus*. London: Penguin Books, 1993.

Sanders, E. P. *Judaism: Practice and Belief: 63 BCE – 66 CE.* Minneapolis: Fortress Press, 2016.

Sanders, E. P. *Paul: The Apostle's Life, Letters, and Thought.* Minneapolis: Fortress Press, 2015.

Sanders, E. P., and Margaret Davies. *Studying the Synoptic Gospels.* London: SCM Press, 1989.

Savage, Luke. "The Kafkaesque Nightmare of Attorney Steven Donziger, a Literal Prisoner of the Chevron Corporation." *Jacobin.* April 2021. https://www.jacobinmag.com/2021/04/attorney-steven-donziger-chevron-ecuador-prosecution-corruption-trial.

Smith, J. Warren. "The Trinity in the Fourth-Century Fathers." In *The Oxford Handbook of the Trinity*, edited by Gilles Emery and Matthew Levering, 109-22. Oxford: Oxford University Press, 2014.

Stark, Thom. *The Human Faces of God: What Scripture Reveals When It Gets God Wrong (and Why Inerrancy Tries To Hide It).* Eugene, OR: Wipf & Stock, 2011.

Stein, Robert H. *Studying the Synoptic Gospels: Origin and Interpretation.* 2nd ed. Grand Rapids: Baker Academic, 2001.

Strobel, Lee. *The Case for Christ: A Journalist's Personal Investigation of the Evidence for Jesus.* Grand Rapids: Zondervan, 1998.

Strobel, Lee. *The Case for the Real Jesus: A Journalist Investigates Current Attacks on the Identity of Christ.* Grand Rapids: Zondervan, 2007.

The Translators to the Readers: Preface to the King James Version of 1611: Unabridged with Original Spelling Retained. Crossreach Publications, 2016.

Tucker, W. Dennis, Jr. "Firmament." In *Eerdmans Dictionary of the Bible*, edited by David Noel Freedman, Allen C. Myers, and Astrid B. Beck. Grand Rapids: William B Eerdmans Publishing Company, 2000.

Van Voorst, Robert E. "Peter, Gospel of." In *Eerdmans Dictionary of the Bible*, edited by David Noel Freedman, Allen C. Myers, and Astrid B. Beck. Grand Rapids: William B Eerdmans Publishing Company, 2000.

Waite, D. A. "The Four-Fold Superiority of the King James Version." AV1611. Accessed November 11, 2021. https://av1611.com/kjbp/articles/waite-fourfold1.html.

Wallace, Daniel B. "Inerrancy and the Text of the New Testament: Assessing the Logic of the Agnostic View." In *Evidence for God: 50 Arguments for Faith from the Bible, History, Philosophy, and Science*, edited by William A. Dembski and Michael R. Licona, 211-19. Grand Rapids: Baker Books, 2010.

Walsh, Anna. "Feds says BPD's claim that gangs formed pact to 'take out' officers was 'non-credible.'" Baltimore Sun. June 24, 2015. https://www.baltimoresun.com/citypaper/bcpnews-feds-say-bpd-s-claim-that-gangs-formed-pact-to-take-out-officers-was-noncredible--20150624-story.html.

Wang, Amy B. "Dubious, curious Arizona place names." AZCentral. August 17, 2014. https://www.azcentral.com/story/news/arizona/2014/08/17/arizona-names-racial-derogatory/14192403.

"William Lane Craig vs Francisco J. Ayala | 'Is Intelligent Design Viable?'" ReasonableFaithOrg video. From a debate recorded at Indiana University on November 5, 2009, https://www.reasonablefaith.org/videos/debates/craig-vs.-ayala-indiana-university.

Wright, N. T. *Evil and the Justice of God.* Downers Grove, IL: InterVarsity Press, 2006.

Wright, N. T. *Jesus and the Victory of God.* Christian Origins and the Question of God. Vol. 2. Minneapolis: Fortress Press, 1996.

Wright, N. T. *The New Testament and the People of God.* Christian Origins and the Question of God. Vol. 1. Minneapolis: Fortress Press, 1992.

Wright, N. T. *Scripture and the Authority of God: How to Read the Bible Today.* New York: HarperOne, 2013.

Wright, N. T. *Simply Christian: Why Christianity Makes Sense.* New York: HarperOne, 2021.

Wright, N. T. *Surprised by Hope: Rethinking Heaven, the Resurrection, and the Mission of the Church.* New York: HarperOne, 2018.

Wright, N. T. *Surprised by Scripture: Engaging Contemporary Issues.* New York: HarperOne, 2015.

Index

About the Author

Dan Kapr holds a Master of Divinity from New Brunswick Theological Seminary, where he graduated magna cum laude. He worked as a youth pastor at Hope Reformed Church in Clifton, New Jersey; Lehman Memorial United Methodist Church in Hatboro, Pennsylvania; and the Community Church in Harrington Park, New Jersey. He also served as a chaplain and assistant camp director at Camp Warwick in Warwick, New York, and performed ministry duties at Harmony Baptist Church, in Middletown, New York. Additionally, he served as a guest preacher at various Reformed churches in New York and New Jersey.

Since losing his Christian faith, Dan has continued to spend much of his time studying philosophy, history, and biblical studies. He ran a blog called *Politely Rejecting Jesus*, which served as the initial concept for this and other planned book projects.

Dan works as a data analyst and is also an experienced stand-up comedian. He has performed in clubs, festivals, and colleges all across the United States. Notable credits include headlining at Eastville Comedy Club in New York, performing at SF Sketchfest, hosting the fifth annual Timmy Awards, and featuring for Tom Myers at the album recording for *Make America Innate Again*. He also spent two miserable days in 2012 working as a carny for the Dutchess County Fair in New York, an experience from which he is still recovering.

Dan currently resides in Pittsburgh, Pennsylvania with his cat Hector. Visit his website at www.dankapr.com.

Printed in Great Britain
by Amazon